I0866554

# AT THE TABLE OF HOLY WISDOM

# AT THE TABLE OF HOLY WISDOM

## Global Hungers and Feminist Biblical Interpretation

BARBARA E. REID, OP

2021 Madeleva Lecture in Spirituality

Paulist Press
New York / Mahwah, NJ

Cover and book design by Lynn Else



Library of Congress Cataloging-in-Publication Data
Names: Reid, Barbara E., author.
Title: At the table of Holy wisdom : global hungers and feminist biblical interpretation / Barbara Reid, OP, 2021 Madeleva Lecture in Spirituality.
Description: New York/Mahwah, NJ : Paulist Press, [2023] | Series: Madeleva lecture in spirituality | Summary: "Feminist liberationist biblical interpretation as a tool for opening the scriptures to women and the disenfranchised"—Provided by publisher.
Identifiers: LCCN 2022041718 (print) | LCCN 2022041719 (ebook) | ISBN 9780809156542 (paperback) | ISBN 9780809188154 (ebook)
Subjects: LCSH: Bible—Feminist criticism. | Liberation theology.
Classification: LCC BS521.4 .R44 2023 (print) | LCC BS521.4 (ebook) | DDC 220.6082—dc23/eng/20221121
LC record available at https://lccn.loc.gov/2022041718
LC ebook record available at https://lccn.loc.gov/2022041719

ISBN 978-0-8091-5654-2 (paperback)
ISBN 978-0-8091-8815-4 (e-book)

Published by Paulist Press
997 Macarthur Boulevard
Mahwah, New Jersey 07430
www.paulistpress.com

Printed and bound in the
United States of America

# CONTENTS

# ABBREVIATIONS

| | |
|---|---|
| AB | Anchor Bible |
| ABRL | Anchor Bible Reference Library |
| AYB | Anchor Yale Bible |
| BCE | Before the Common Era |
| BDAG | Walter Bauer, Frederick William Danker, William Arndt, F. Wilbur Gingrich, *A Greek-English Lexicon of the New Testament and Other Early Christian Literature*, 3rd ed. (Chicago: University of Chicago Press, 2001). |
| BibInt | Biblical Interpretation series |
| *BibRev* | *Bible Review* |
| BJS | Brown Judaic Studies |
| BZNW | Beihefte zur Zeitschrift für die neutestamentliche Wissenschaft |
| *CBQ* | *Catholic Biblical Quarterly* |
| CE | Common Era |
| *DRev* | *Downside Review* |
| FCNTECW | Feminist Companion to the New Testament and Early Christian Writings |
| *HeyJ* | *Heythrop Journal* |

| | |
|---|---|
| *HTR* | *Harvard Theological Review* |
| IFT | Introductions in Feminist Theology |
| *JBL* | *Journal of Biblical Literature* |
| JSNTSup | Journal for the Study of the New Testament Supplement Series |
| KJV | King James Version |
| NABRE | New American Bible Revised Edition |
| NASB | New American Standard Bible |
| NEB | New English Bible |
| *Neot* | *Neotestamentica* |
| NIV | New International Version |
| NJB | New Jerusalem Bible |
| *NovT* | *Novum Testamentum* |
| NRSV | New Revised Standard Version |
| *NTS* | *New Testament Studies* |
| OECS | Oxford Early Christian Studies |
| RSV | Revised Standard Version |
| SP | *Sacra Pagina* |
| SymS | Symposium Series |
| WCS | Wisdom Commentary series |
| WUNT | Wissenschaftliche Untersuchungen zum Neuen Testament |
| *ZNW* | *Zeitschrift für die neutestamentliche Wissenschaft und die Kunde der älteren Kirche* |

# INTRODUCTION

Sister Madeleva Wolff, former president of St. Mary's College, founded the first School of Sacred Theology open to women in June 1943. For more than a decade afterward, this was the only place in the world where a layperson, male or female, religious or lay, could earn an advanced degree in Catholic theology. Such creativity and courage continue to inspire us as we face unprecedented challenges in our day.

Sister Madeleva is said to have been inspired by audacious women in the Old Testament. Perhaps among them was Woman Wisdom, who invites all to her banquet: "Come, eat of my bread and drink of the wine I have mixed. Lay aside immaturity and live and walk in the way of insight" (Prov 9:5–6). Eating at Wisdom's banquet is an image for the nourishing teaching she offers, intended to guide those who partake of it into living wisely and well. We come to Wisdom's table famished: after this exhausting time of worldwide pandemic, of gut-wrenching divisions in our country and throughout the globe, of heightened awareness of deep-seated racism, of the waves of desperate migrants and refugees, of peril for our planet, we hunger for well-being for all, for comfort after all the losses; for oneness, justice, equity, and inclusion for all peoples, for the flourishing of all creation. And those who are hungriest and have the hardest time getting a place at the table are women and children, especially those of color.

In what follows, I will explore how feminist liberationist biblical interpretation gives us one of many essential tools needed to alleviate these hungers. First, I invite you to reflect on Woman Wisdom's way of cooking, then on getting a place at the table, on seating arrangements, and finally, on reshaping the table.

I

# LEARNING TO COOK FOR A FEAST WITH WOMAN WISDOM

When people are starving, we cannot offer them empty calories. Our Scriptures provide rich, savory, filling fare—if they're served properly. But there is also poison that we need to learn to identify and refuse to serve. Recipes from a feminist liberative approach to the Scriptures can offer the kind of nourishment Woman Wisdom would want to give, as she makes a place for all at her table.

## A FEMINIST FEAST

First, I want to define what I mean by *feminist*: it is "a perspective and a movement that springs from a recognition of inequities toward women, and it advocates for changes in whatever structures prevent full flourishing of all creation."[1] Feminists recognize that not only gender but also race, class, and culture are all determinative factors that shape our experience and understanding. To call attention to the double oppression of racism and sexism, African American feminists have adopted the term *womanist*.[2] Similarly, some Latinas use *mujerista* (*mujer* is Spanish for "woman") or "Latina feminist" to highlight the context for their theologizing as *mestizaje* and *mulatez* (racial and cultural mixture), done *en conjunto* (in community), with *lo cotidiano* (everyday lived experience) of Latinas as starting points for theological reflection and the encounter with the divine. As a gender-neutral or nonbinary alternative, many today use *Latinx*.[3] Men and those who identify in nonbinary ways are also welcome in Holy Wisdom's culinary school. While men may not experience gender discrimination in the same way women do, they can choose to identify with and accompany us in learning to serve a feminist feast.

## GATHERING THE INGREDIENTS

The first step in feminist biblical interpretation is to gather the essential ingredients that come from the experiences of women and other disadvantaged persons.[4] One does not begin with the biblical text, but with real life.[5] To acquire this ingredient, we need to pay attention to women's experiences of gender discrimination as well as to inequities based on race, culture, class, age, ethnicity, and other social markers. As well, we reflect on the experiences of liberation and how those are fostered. There is no universal "women's experience," so this ingredient must be gathered from women in many different contexts around the globe.

## WHOSE KITCHEN?

The next step is to recognize that it makes a difference whose kitchen you're cooking in. That is, to cook up a feast with Holy Wisdom, it is necessary to identify one's social location and to be conscious of how that influences what one sees in lived reality and in the biblical text. For example, in Matthew's parable of the workers in the vineyard (20:1–16), a person of privilege will likely identify with the laborers who worked all day in the hot sun. Such a reader may struggle with questions of entitlement and perceived injustice when the owner decides to pay everyone the same amount at the end of the day. However, a person with few professional skills who struggles to get meaningful work may identify with the last hired and might hear in the parable a reassuring message that God's beneficence is freely given to all and not something earned.

A participant in a workshop I once gave on the parables told me that she resonated with the last hired. A single mother with limited education and skills and who tried day after day to find a job, she saw the day laborers standing in the marketplace as those who wanted to work but kept being passed over because they looked weak, old, or sick, and so the vineyard owner only chose them when there was no one left. When the master paid each the same amount, regardless of the length of time they worked, she saw this as a metaphor for

God's justice—giving to all freely and equally, not based on how long each worked, but on the need for all to eat at the end of the day. She observed that if the owner gave those hired later less than a denarius—the amount needed to feed their family for a day—what good would that be? She further noted that the ones who worked all day, although they had endured longer hours of work under the hot sun, had the satisfaction of knowing all day that they would be able to feed their family at the end of the day. What she saw was that godly justice meant all deserved to eat, regardless of how much they worked. From my privileged perspective of never having gone hungry or without meaningful work, I never would have seen that message in the parable. I had to step into another woman's kitchen to see what she perceived, which was likely much closer to what Galilean peasants in the time of Jesus heard in the parable the first time he told it.

## OLD FAMILY RECIPES

Another critical step is to scrutinize the origin of the recipes (the biblical texts and their interpretations) that have been handed down to us. We ask questions such as: Who wrote the text and for whom? Where? In what circumstances? With what intent? Unfortunately, our biblical books don't come with identifying labels that will answer these questions with complete assurance. We can make some approximations. But most important, from a feminist perspective, is to acknowledge that the various books of the Bible have been written, for the most part, by men, for men, about men, and to serve men's interests. In addition, until recent decades, most of the biblical commentaries, sermons, and Bible studies have been produced by white, Western, educated men. Therefore, feminists ask questions that try to unearth: What were the experiences of women and other disadvantaged persons in biblical times? In our time? How would they have told the story? What meaning did they derive from it? Feminists ask these questions not only of the biblical text, but also of those preachers, teachers, and scholarly commentators who have passed on to us their interpretations.

## HOW MANY CALORIES?

Another important step is to evaluate who is nourished by the text and who is left hungry. Does the text provide nutrient-dense food? Does acceptance of it lead to flourishing of life? Or does it offer empty calories, upholding systems of domination and oppression? For example, Paul's admonition, "Wives, be subject to your husbands" (Col 3:18), can be taken to heart by a woman who is in an abusive relationship as divine justification for her to submit meekly to beatings by her partner rather than try to stop the violence. Clearly, interiorizing such a message is contrary to the liberating message Jesus proclaimed. A feminist cook would challenge the kyriarchal[6] household model accepted unquestioningly in Paul's day, which no longer serves in contemporary societies in which spouses work toward equitable sharing of household responsibilities and authority.

## EXPERIMENTING WITH NEW RECIPES

Woman Wisdom invites her pupils to unleash all their powers of creative imagination to dream of a world in which there is equality and dignity for all. Being able to envision such a world then gives the energy to create it. Drama, art, music, dance, storytelling, and ritual can all help to unleash the creative powers that can move us from dreaming to actuality.

## A NOT-SO-SECRET INGREDIENT

A not-so-secret ingredient is the presence of women from the beginning of the biblical story. However, not all interpreters of Scripture are aware of it, or how to retrieve it. Feminists use all the best tools of historical-critical exegesis to reconstruct women's experience from biblical times, remembering that women have always been central to discipleship and mission. We bring forward women who are in the text who have been overlooked or forgotten. And when women are not mentioned, we continually ask: Where were they? What were their experiences? When women are mentioned, such as Phoebe, "deacon of the church at Cenchreae" (Rom 16:1), and Junia, "prominent among the apostles" (Rom 16:7), we surmise that they are merely the tip of the iceberg; there must have been many more women deacons and apostles whose names are now lost to us. Another important strategy is to distinguish between description and prescription. For example, when Paul says, "Women should be silent in the churches" (1 Cor 14:34), we recognize that he is prescribing what he wants to happen, not describing actual practice, for we see from 11:2–11 in the very same letter, that women did speak in the assembly, prophesying and praying, without censure. A feminist cook would want to investigate what kinds of speech are acceptable to whom in the assembly and which are not; who wanted the women to be silent and why.

## DISCARDING WHAT'S EXPIRED

Retrieval of the stories and traditions that are laudatory of women and other disadvantaged persons is very important. But just as important is the remembrance of the "texts of terror," as Phyllis Trible so aptly named the biblical stories that describe and seem to accept or even laud unspeakable violence toward women, such as the abuse and dismemberment of the unnamed concubine of the Levite in Judges 19.[7] At first, we might be tempted to erase and bury such stories—discarding them as expired, no longer having any food value. But a feminist liberative approach urges us to remember and repeat them, not to perpetuate their brutality, but to expose such tales that approve violence toward women and other disadvantaged persons and denounce them, insisting, "Never again!"

## READY TO SERVE

The final stage, of course, is to serve the meal, that is, to take action toward transformation. Feminist biblical interpretation is far more than an intellectual exercise. Having begun with analyzing women's realities, it comes full circle to take actions that will impact those realities, trying to correct injustices. Such actions work for change on two levels: in personal relationship patterns and on the systemic level—to work to dismantle structures that keep domination and inequity in place.

The ingredients of feminist biblical interpretation that we have sketched out can give us a basic recipe, but they are not a formula that, if followed exactly, will give us a correct or liberative meaning once and for all. Biblical interpretation is an art, and the recipes and the meals must be adapted to each context. If we shift our metaphor from cooking to dancing, Elisabeth Schüssler Fiorenza likens the movements of feminist liberationist biblical interpretation to a dance where the steps interweave one another in various patterns.[8] It is a lively tango that can energize us for a new world and church. One caution, however: Wisdom's feast is not just a spicier, tastier version of what's been served up before; Woman Wisdom would not have you just "add woman and stir." Rather, a whole new way of cooking, serving, and ingesting is needed—a retraining of the tastebuds, where any vestiges of biblical interpretation that exalts clericalism, domination, and submission, or violence toward defenseless persons, creatures, or Earth, are spat out as vile poisons we can no longer consume.

## NOTABLE CHEFS

Women have always cooked up their own interpretations of the Bible, bringing the word to life for their family and faith communities.[9] Many of these "chefs" remain unknown. Following are brief sketches of some of the notable forerunners in feminist biblical interpretation.[10] One of the earliest known Christian women who challenged patriarchal interpretations of Scripture was Helie, a consecrated virgin, who lived in the second century CE. When her parents and a judge tried to force her to marry, quoting St. Paul: "It is better to marry than to be aflame with passion" (1 Cor 7:9), she retorted, "But not so for everyone, that is, not for holy virgins."[11] She rightly points out that a text does not have only one meaning that can be applied in all situations.

Another woman who lived in the second century, Beruriah, whose husband was a respected rabbi, was said to have equally "profound knowledge of biblical exegesis and outstanding intelligence."[12] The Talmud preserves a story of an instance when she challenged her husband as he prayed for the destruction of a sinner. She offered instead that Psalm 104:35 urged them to pray for the destruction of sin, not the sinner (b. Ber. 10a).

It is not until medieval times that the first written commentaries on Scripture written from what today we would call a feminist critical point of view emerge. If such works existed earlier, they are lost to us now. Among the earliest are those of Hildegard of Bingen (1098–1179), German writer, mystic, and abbess of a Benedictine monastery. She wrote authoritatively of her experiences of God as revealed in prayer, speaking of the Divine as feminine.[13] In her interpretations of Genesis, she saw women and men as complementary and interdependent.

Also important in this era were women scribes who copied biblical manuscripts. Paula Dei Mansi of Verona is a notable example. She came from a distinguished family of Jewish scribes. In 1288, she not only translated her father's commentaries on Scripture from Hebrew to Italian but also added her own explanations.[14]

Another pioneer was French court writer and poet Christine de Pizan (ca. 1365–1430). She challenged misogynistic readings of Scripture, using allegory and common sense. In addition, she lifted up the accomplishments of women in the Bible to advocate for women taking active roles in society in her day.[15]

By the seventeenth century, there were women who insisted that the biblical text be understood and interpreted in its historical context, not applied in a literal fashion to all times and places. Many of them, like Margaret Fell,[16] questioned Pauline texts, such as 1 Corinthians 14:34–36, which prohibits women from speaking in church.

In the eighteenth and nineteenth centuries, some women began to challenge interpretations of Scripture based on faulty translations of the Hebrew and Greek. Sarah (1792–1873) and Angelina (1805–1879) Grimké, Quakers from a slaveholding family in South Carolina, became strong public advocates for the abolition of slavery and for women's rights. When men tried to silence them, claiming the Bible prohibited women from speaking in public (e.g., 1 Cor 14:34), they took to studying the original languages, Hebrew and Greek, so they could interpret the Bible for themselves.[17] Another prominent abolitionist, Isabella Baumfree (who adopted the name Sojourner Truth), a former slave and powerful preacher, quoted the Bible liberally in her speeches. Her most famous speech, "Ain't I a Woman?" given in 1851 at the Ohio Women's Rights Convention, exemplifies how she confronted cultural assumptions and biblical interpretations that support gender inequities.[18]

Another monumental work that emerged in the nineteenth century was *The Women of Israel*, published in 1845 by Jewish theologian Grace Aguilar (1816–1847).[19] Her aim was to show the relevance of the biblical women to contemporary Jewish women's concerns and to see women in the Scriptures as a source of strength and encouragement. Moreover, she wanted to combat anti-Jewish strains in emerging Christian feminism, where the notion prevailed that Jewish law degraded women whereas Christianity upheld their dignity and value. Such a mistaken notion is still among the poisons that feminist chefs must assiduously avoid. Aguilar's work is notable for its lifting up of every female character in the Bible, even the most obscure.[20]

The first full-blown feminist commentary on the Bible was written by Elizabeth Cady Stanton (1815–1902), a leader in the suffragist movement in the United States. She encountered the same thing the Grimké sisters and others experienced: the Bible was constantly being quoted to stop women from making inroads into politics, education, or the work world. So Cady Stanton, along with several other women, set about producing a biblical commentary on every text that concerned women. They produced two volumes entitled *The Woman's Bible* (1895 and 1898), urging women to recognize that texts and interpretations that degrade women come from men, not from God. They advocated using common sense to rethink what had been presented to them as sacred.

Nearly a century later, Carol A. Newsom and Sharon H. Ringe produced *The Women's Bible Commentary* (Westminster John Knox, 1992), a one-volume commentary on those passages in the Protestant canon deemed relevant to women. The authors are feminists primarily from North America. Six years later, they revised and expanded the work to include a greater diversity of feminist authors from around the globe, and the Apocrypha/Deuterocanonical books were added. The third edition, which came out in 2012, reflects the profound advances made in feminist biblical scholarship and includes newer voices. Recognizing the proliferation of feminist commentaries on the Scriptures, "The" has been dropped from the title of the second and third editions.

Another work that appeared at the centennial of Cady Stanton's commentaries is Elisabeth Schüssler Fiorenza's two-volume project *Searching the Scriptures*, produced with the assistance of Shelly Matthews.[21] The first volume is devoted to method, charting a comprehensive approach to feminist interpretation with essays from diverse ecumenical, interreligious, and multicultural perspectives. The second contains critical feminist commentary by scholars from around the globe on each book of the New Testament as well as on three books of Jewish Pseudepigraph and eleven other early Christian writings.

Similar work was being undertaken in Europe, for example, with ***Kompendium Feministische Bibelauslegung***, edited by Luise Schottroff and Marie-Theres Wacker, which was published in 2007. This one-volume commentary features German feminist biblical interpretation of each book of the Bible, along with apocryphal books and several extrabiblical texts. Now in its third edition, it has recently been translated into English.[22] A multivolume project ***The Bible and Women: An Encyclopaedia of Exegesis and Cultural History***, edited by Irmtraud Fischer, Adriana Valerio, Mercedes Navarro Puerto, Christiana de Groot, and Mary Ann Beavis, is underway. This project presents a history of the reception of the Bible as embedded in Western cultural history and focuses particularly on gender-relevant biblical themes, biblical female characters, and women recipients of the Bible. To date, ten volumes are available in English; sixteen in German; nine in Italian; and twelve in Spanish.[23]

Another significant collection is the Feminist Companion to the Bible series, edited by Athalya Brenner (Sheffield: Sheffield Academic, 1993–2015). Each of the twenty volumes comprises essays on select portions of the Old Testament. The parallel series on the New Testament and Early Christian Writings, edited by Amy-Jill Levine with Marianne Blickenstaff and Maria Mayo

Robbins, has thirteen volumes, published between 2001 and 2009.

In 2015, the first of sixty volumes of ***Wisdom Commentary*** series was published. This is the first series to provide comprehensive critical feminist biblical interpretation of every part of every book of the Bible. It reflects the significant shifts over the decades from focusing on passages where there are female characters, to now analyzing every part of the text for both its promise and pitfalls regarding women and other vulnerable persons as well as our endangered creation. The editors, led by myself, are a team of Roman Catholic, Protestant, and Jewish biblical scholars and include ground-breaking methods and voices of feminist women and men from around the world (see www.wisdomcommentary.org).

Returning to our cooking metaphor, the number of feminist cooks and their recipes are now too numerous to list. In times gone by, the women listed above as notable early "chefs" and others like them shared their recipes informally with one another, but most of their wisdom is now lost to us. Until recent decades, the only ones admitted to the "culinary schools" for formal training in academic biblical scholarship were men. They were the only ones who wrote the cookbooks and taught others to cook. Now with women taking their rightful place in the academy and in pastoral settings, new recipes and new flavors shared around the globe are feeding people everywhere who are hungry for a nourishing word.

# II

# A PLACE AT THE TABLE

Now we're ready to come to the table. Feminists today use the expression "getting a place at the table" to speak about the necessity for women to be included in the places where important discussions and decisions take place. Not only in the church, but in business, politics, and all other arenas of power from which women have been excluded, there are persistent calls for women to take their place at the table.[1] In March 1943, Sister Madeleva, in her ninth year as president at St. Mary's College, was appointed to head a subcommittee of the National Catholic Education Association to address the problem of Catholic sisters being asked to teach religion without proper preparation. No university would accept them into their theology programs; only priests need apply. And so, Sister Madeleva created St. Mary's School of Theology for women to get a place at the table.

We see in our day small but significant advances: on January 20, 2021, the first female woman of color was sworn in as Vice President of the United States; in February 2021, Pope Francis appointed Sister Nathalie Becquart to serve as Under Secretary at the Vatican's Synod of Bishops and Catia Summaria to serve as a prosecutor in the Vatican Court of Appeal; in March 2021, Sister Nuria Calduch-Benages was appointed secretary of the Pontifical Biblical Commission. These are just a few of the increasing number of women who are breaking stained glass ceilings each year. Yet there remain many tables that boast signs such as "reserved for men" or better, "for ordained celibate men only." Some of the reasons for exclusion of women rest on inadequate or even faulty interpretations of the Bible.

## ONLY TWELVE PLACE SETTINGS?

Despite decades of work by feminist biblical scholars and theologians, in the minds of many Christian believers, the only ones who accompanied Jesus throughout his earthly ministry and to whom he entrusted the mission after his death were twelve male apostles.[2] And in the imaginations of many Christians, only the twelve men were at the table with Jesus when he shared his Last Supper with them where he supposedly "ordained" them. That believers conflate ***disciples***, ***apostles***, and ***the Twelve*** is understandable, given the way some of the evangelists intertwine them. In the next sections, we will examine the differences between disciples, apostles, and the Twelve. Although no women are named among the Twelve, there are clear indications that there were women disciples and apostles.

We begin with *disciples*, the term that occurs the most often of the three and the one that describes the largest group. The noun *mathētēs*, "disciple," means "pupil, apprentice, adherent,"[3] and is used very frequently in each of the Gospels.[4] Certain characters are explicitly named disciples: Peter, Judas, James and John, Joseph of Arimathea, Andrew, Philip, Thomas, and Nathanael.[5] One woman is explicitly named a disciple: Tabitha (Acts 9:36), with the feminine form, *mathētria*. There is one other instance where there may be a reference to Mary Magdalene as a disciple. At John 21:14, after Jesus appears to Simon Peter, Thomas, Nathaniel, the sons of Zebedee, and two other disciples by the Sea of Tiberias, the evangelist comments, "This was now the third time that Jesus appeared to the disciples after he was raised from the dead." As the Gospel now stands, this is actually the fourth appearance: the first was to Mary Magdalene (20:11–18); then that same evening to the disciples who were behind locked doors (20:19–23); then a week later to Thomas (20:26–29). Many commentators overlook the appearance to Mary Magdalene, supposing that *disciples* refers only to males. Or they argue that the precise term *disciple* is not found in John 20:11–18 as it is at 20:19; 20:26; and 21:1, 2, 4, 14.[6] Adele Reinhartz offers another explanation: "The Johannine narrative is not always consistent in its enumeration. John 4:54 refers to the healing of the nobleman's son as the second sign that Jesus did after coming from Judea to Galilee, though it would seem that in fact this healing was Jesus' third sign as narrated in the gospel."[7]

The instances in which named characters are called disciples are few. In most occurrences, the noun is plural, *hoi mathētai*, with no indication whether the *disciples* are comprised of men, women, or both. When we examine what characterizes discipleship, it becomes abundantly clear that women were among Jesus's disciples.

None of the Gospels defines how one qualifies for discipleship. Many scholars would concur with the three criteria listed by John Meier in his monumental work, *A Marginal Jew*:

> (1) A disciple is one called by Jesus with a command to follow him; (2) "following" was not metaphorical, but literal and physical; those who accepted his command to follow had to leave behind home, family, and other comfortable ties; (3) on top of these hardships, Jesus warned his disciples that they might face other sufferings: hostility and even deadly opposition, including opposition from one's own alienated family.[8]

With these criteria, Meier sees Peter, Andrew, James, John, Levi, and Nathaniel qualifying as disciples. And he recognizes that "the Gospels present us with a picture of women traveling with Jesus, supporting and serving Jesus out of their own means, and standing by Jesus at his crucifixion when most if not all of his male disciples deserted him—and what should qualify for discipleship if not such steadfast service and loyalty to Jesus even unto the cross?"[9] Nonetheless, because the word "'disciple' is never applied to any of these women or to the whole group of women followers when they are mentioned apart from the male followers"[10] and because there are no call stories of women in the Gospels, Meier concludes that there were women disciples in reality, but not in name.[11] This conclusion warrants reconsideration when we look at the ways in which women in the Gospels fulfill the criteria Meier delineates. Moreover, there are other criteria for discipleship that we can deduce from Jesus's instructions to his disciples.[12] These include: being called, following Jesus, serving, offering hospitality, hearing and acting on the Word, giving up family and possessions, taking up the cross, and being like the Teacher.

## *Being Called*

The fact that there are no call stories of women disciples preserved in the Gospels does not mean that no women were called by Jesus or that such stories did not circulate in the early church. The Gospel writers were selective in the material they included. Below we will explore the possibility first put forward by Elaine M. Wainwright, that behind the Matthean version of the healing of Simon's mother-in-law (Matt 8:14–15) there lay a call story with a healing motif.[13] In addition, the story of the annunciation to Mary (Luke 1:26–38) exhibits all the characteristics of a call story (see the section below, "*Diakonia*: More than Table Service"). We also note that for two of the characters explicitly named disciples, there are no call stories: Joseph of Arimathea (Matt 27:57; John 19:38) and Tabitha (Acts 9:36).

### *Following Jesus*

The Synoptic evangelists clearly say that Galilean women followed Jesus. In Mark's crucifixion scene, he names three and adds that there were many others: "Mary Magdalene, and Mary the mother of James the younger and of Joses, and Ṣalome…used to follow him [*ēkolouthoun autǭ*] and provided for him [*diēkonoun autǭ*] when he was in Galilee; and there were many other women who had come up with him to Jerusalem" (Mark 15:40–41). In Matthew's parallel account, he starts by saying there were many women and then singles out two by name: "Many women were also there, looking on from a distance; they had followed [*ēkolouthēsan*] Jesus from Galilee and had provided for him. Among them were Mary Magdalene, and Mary the mother of James and Joseph, and the mother of the sons of Zebedee" (Matt 27:55–56).

In Mark and Matthew, these women followers do not appear explicitly until the end of the story. These two evangelists make it clear, however, that they have been there all along, using verbs in the imperfect tense to indicate that the women's following and ministering were ongoing repeated past actions (Mark 15:40–41; similarly, Matt 27:55).[14]

Luke introduces the women disciples much earlier in the narrative. At Luke 8:1–3, Jesus is traveling "through cities and villages, proclaiming and bringing the good news of the kingdom of God. The twelve were with him, as well as some women who had been cured of evil spirits and infirmities: Mary, called Magdalene, from whom seven demons had gone out, and Joanna, the wife of Herod's steward Chuza, and Susanna, and many others, who provided for them [*diēkonoun autois*] out of their resources."[15] In the Lukan crucifixion scene, the women "who had followed [*synakolouthousai*] him from Galilee" (23:49) are still with him, although Luke dilutes their importance, adding "all his acquaintances" as witnesses. The women continue to follow when Joseph of Arimathea entombs the body: "the women who had come with him from Galilee followed [*katakolouthēsasai*], and they saw the tomb and how his body was laid" (23:55). Not until the scene at the empty tomb does Luke give any of the women's names and, like Mark and Matthew, he notes that there were others: "Mary Magdalene, Joanna, Mary the mother of James, and the other women with them" (24:10).

## *Serving*

In the instances noted above, following is linked with serving (*diakonein*). This juxtaposition is found in the Fourth Gospel as well, where Jesus says, "Whoever serves [*diakonę̄*] me must follow [*akoloutheitō*] me, and where I am, there will my servant [*ho diakonos*] be also" (John 12:26). In all four Gospels, Jesus gives instructions to his disciples about serving, pointing to his own example, for instance, "For the Son of Man came not to be served [*diakonēthēnai*] but to serve [*diakonēsai*], and to give his life a ransom for many" (Mark 10:45 // Matt 20:28).[16] It is apparent that serving is another characteristic of discipleship. We will explore all the female characters in the Gospels and Acts who are associated with serving in the next section.

## *Offering Hospitality*

Another criterion for discipleship is offering hospitality. In Matthew 18:5 and parallels, Jesus instructs his disciples:[17] "Whoever welcomes one such child in my name welcomes me." And in the parable of the final judgment, Jesus tells his disciples[18] that those who are blessed and who will inherit the kingdom are the ones who welcomed the stranger (25:35). In the Gospel of John, at the crucifixion, Jesus entrusts his mother to the disciple whom he loved (19:26), "and from that hour the disciple took her into his own home" (John 19:27). Although the vocabulary varies in the different accounts, the action is the same: receiving, welcoming, extending hospitality. Women who exemplify hospitality and who could then be characterized as disciples include: Martha, who "welcomed him [Jesus] into her home" (Luke 10:38), Lydia, who prevailed upon Paul and his companions to stay at her home (Acts 16:15, 40), and women such as Mary, the mother of John Mark (Acts 12:12), Prisca (Rom 16:5), and Nympha (Col 4:15), who hosted house churches.[19]

### *Hearing and Acting on the Word*

One other criterion for discipleship is listening to and learning the teachings of Jesus; as indeed, the basic meaning of *mathētēs* is "learner" or "student." There is a strong emphasis in the Gospels that learning Jesus's teachings entails putting them into practice. In the Synoptic Gospels, the parable of the seed that bears abundant fruit when sown on good soil illustrates the point of what happens when a disciple hears the word and acts on it (Mark 4:20 // Matt 13:23 // Luke 8:15).[20] In Luke, Jesus's new "family" of disciples "are those who hear the word of God and do it" (11:28). Similarly, in the Gospel of John, Jesus says to the Jews who had believed in him, "If you continue in my word, you are truly my disciples" (8:31). A prime example of one who listens to the word and puts it into practice is Mary, Jesus's mother, as portrayed in Luke's first chapter. After listening to Gabriel, she responds, "Here I am the servant of the Lord; let it be with me according to your word" (Luke 1:38).

### *Giving Up Family and Possessions, Taking Up the Cross*

The Third Evangelist adds these criteria that emphasize the cost of following Jesus: "Whoever comes to me and does not hate father and mother, wife and children, brothers and sisters, yes, and even life itself, cannot be my disciple. Whoever does not carry the cross and follow me cannot be my disciple…none of you can become my disciple if you do not give up all your possessions" (14:26–27, 29). This saying insists that for a disciple, Jesus and his mission must take priority over all else, even what one holds most dear: family, possessions, and one's very life. The new family of disciples takes precedence over blood kin.[21] In Mark's Gospel, there is a sharp distinction between the two (Mark 3:31–35; similarly, Matt 12:48–50); Luke, however, allows that Jesus's mother and siblings are among those who hear the Word and put it into practice (Luke 1:38; 8:21). Likewise, in the Gospel of John, blood kin of Jesus and disciples can both belong to the community of disciples, as seen in the crucifixion scene, where Jesus entrusts his mother (symbolizing those bound to Jesus by blood ties) to the Beloved Disciple (symbolizing all those who are tied to Jesus by believing in him) and vice versa (19:25–27).

We know very little about the marital status of the women named in the Gospels, aside from Joanna (married to Chuza, Luke 8:3) and Prisca (married to Aquila, Acts 18:2), and those identified as widows (e.g., Anna, Luke 2:36–37) and numerous unnamed widows. It is curious that when most biblical women are identified by their relationship to a man (their father, husband, or son), such is not the case with a number of the women disciples, such as Mary Magdalene, Susanna, Mary and Martha,[22] Lydia, and Phoebe. We do not know whether they were single, married, divorced, widowed, or how their discipleship affected their relationships with the men in their lives. We do not know how, precisely, the women disciples would have prioritized the family of disciples over their own blood kin. Outside the Gospels, there are many traditions in the early church of women disciples who refused to marry or who left their husbands to go out and preach the gospel.[23] We can only speculate whether some of the women disciples named in the New Testament did likewise.

All the Synoptic Gospels have a similar instruction from Jesus: that anyone who wants to be a disciple must take up their cross and follow him (Mark 8:34; Matt 10:38; 16:24; Luke 9:23; 14:27). Willingness to "take up their cross" is a way of saying that disciples must be prepared to accept negative consequences for their following Jesus and living by his teachings. Jesus is not asking his followers to accept and bear every kind of suffering, especially that which results from evil actions or systemic injustices. Disciples are to root out the sources of that kind of suffering wherever possible, as did Jesus. "Taking up the cross" refers to a specific kind of suffering—the repercussions disciples can experience as a result of their adherence to Jesus.[24] In Jesus's day, such repercussions could include divisions in the family (Luke 12:53), loss of status and influence for those who were rich (Luke 14:12–14), arrest, persecution, or betrayal by family members and friends, and even death (Luke 21:12, 16–17). Exposing oneself to carrying such crosses must be a freely chosen stance for a disciple.

In the Gospels, no disciple is depicted as suffering for following Jesus, although the women who keep watch at the crucifixion were certainly putting themselves at risk and would have suffered mental anguish witnessing Jesus's execution. In the Gospel of Luke, Simeon prophesies to Mary, the mother of Jesus, about the suffering she will endure. He speaks to her of the sword that will pierce her soul (Luke 2:35). Joseph Fitzmyer understands the sword that is to pass through Mary's soul not as a reference to the anguish she will experience as she sees Jesus crucified, but as an allusion to the sword of discrimination in Ezekiel 14:17 and that Simeon "hints at the difficulty she will have in learning that obedience to the word of God will transcend even family ties."[25] Either way, there is suffering involved. The Fourth Evangelist clearly depicts Mary witnessing her son's crucifixion (John 19:25–27), truly one of the most anguishing experiences a mother could have.[26]

Vivid accounts of the dangerous consequences of discipleship are abundant in the Acts of the Apostles. Stephen is stoned to death (Acts 7:54–60), and Herod has James the brother of John killed by the sword (12:2). Peter is imprisoned (4:3; 12:4); Paul and his companions endure repeated beatings, imprisonments, and many other hardships as a result of their preaching (e.g., 14:5, 19; 16:19–24; 21:27–40).[27] Although no female characters are shown to suffer in this way, Luke twice notes that before his own transformation into a disciple, Saul persecuted both women and men. Immediately following the stoning and burial of Stephen, "Saul was ravaging the church by entering house after house; dragging off both men and women, he committed them to prison" (8:3). And after Philip's encounter with the Ethiopian eunuch, Saul was "still breathing threats and murder against the disciples of the Lord, went to the high priest and asked him for letters to the synagogues at Damascus, so that if he found any who belonged to the Way, men or women, he might bring them bound to Jerusalem" (Acts 9:1–2). There is one reference to a woman who exposes herself to danger for the sake of the gospel in Paul's letter to the Romans. Paul comments that his coworkers Prisca and Aquila "risked their necks" for his life (Rom 16:4).

One of the ways in which radical self-emptying is evident in disciples is their use of possessions. Luke emphasizes this more than the other evangelists, going so far as to have Jesus say that one cannot be a disciple without giving up all their possessions (14:33). While there are disciples who are said to have left everything behind to follow Jesus (Simon Peter, James, John, and Levi/Matthew (Luke 5:11, 28 and pars.), others, such as Mary Magdalene, Joanna, Susanna, and other Galilean women use their possessions to finance Jesus's mission (Luke 8:1–3). Another way is exemplified by Zacchaeus, a wealthy chief tax collector, who gives half his possessions to the poor (Luke 19:1–10). Yet another way is depicted in the Acts of the Apostles. The early community of Jesus's disciples in Jerusalem held all things in common and "would sell their possessions and goods and distribute the proceeds to all, as any had need" (Acts 2:44) so that "there was not a needy person among them" (Acts 4:34).[28]

What we see is that there is a variety of ways in which disciples express their commitment to Jesus. There is no uniform formula for living out discipleship. The one constant is that disciples exhibit a radical letting go that frees the heart and ensures that all have what they need to thrive. A vivid image of such total self-gift is the widow who gave her whole life when she deposited two small coins into the temple treasury. Jesus comments to his disciples, "Truly I tell you, this poor widow has put in more than all those who are contributing to the treasury. For all of them have contributed out of their abundance; but she out of her poverty has put in everything she had, all she had to live on [*holon ton bion autēs*]" (Mark 12:43–44; similarly, Luke 21:1–4). This translation in the NRSV does not capture well the nuance of the Greek *bios*, which means not only livelihood, but life itself. The widow is an icon of the total gift of self exemplified by Jesus: she gave her whole life, not simply "all she had to live on."

### *Being Like the Teacher*

One final characteristic of disciples is that they will be like their teacher, as Jesus declares in his Sermon on the Plain (Luke 6:40; cf. Matt 10:25). One way of being like the teacher is to teach. In the Gospels, it is Jesus who teaches; it is not until Acts that the disciples are shown as doing as their teacher did.[29] While most of the examples in Acts are male, one female teacher stands out: Priscilla.[30] In Acts 18, she and her husband Aquila host Paul in Corinth and then set sail with him to Ephesus.

Paul left them there to carry on the mission, while he went on to Caesarea, Jerusalem, Antioch, and beyond. Meanwhile, Priscilla and Aquila encounter an eloquent preacher, Apollos, who hailed from Alexandria. He was well versed in the Scriptures "and taught accurately the things concerning Jesus, though he knew only the baptism of John" (18:25). Linda Maloney explains, "In other words, he knew of the Jewish practice of 'baptism for repentance' or for purification, but he was unaware of the new baptism into the Way, which confers the Holy Spirit."[31] After Priscilla and Aquila heard him speaking in the synagogue, "they took him aside and explained the Way of God to him more accurately" (18:26), that is, they "described how the Jesus movement had developed post-Easter and what the Pentecost events signified."[32] This is an extraordinary depiction of a woman teacher who is more advanced in her understanding than the prominent preacher Apollos, and who instructs him—and that he evidently received it to good effect.[33] That Priscilla is named ahead of her husband[34] indicates her prominence and status. In Paul's letters we catch further glimpses of how Prisca enacted her discipleship. She and Aquila are a missionary couple who are coworkers (*synergoi*)[35] of Paul, "risked their necks" for him, and host the church in their house (Rom 16:3–5; 1 Cor 16:19).

From the above discussion, it is evident that there are multiple criteria for discipleship that can be derived from Jesus's instructions to his disciples. They include: being called, following, serving, offering hospitality, hearing and acting on the Word, being willing to place the demands of discipleship above one's own family, possessions, and even one's life, being willing to expose oneself to the negative consequences of following Jesus's Way, and emulating the Teacher. Examples of women who fulfill these characteristics are plentiful in the Gospels and Acts. In most instances, "the disciples" occurs in the plural, ***hoi mathētai***, with no indication of their gender. When we encounter "the disciples," we should envision both women and men being taught by Jesus and adhering to his way of life—Jesus's table was set for far more than twelve men.[36]

In the next section we will explore in more detail the ways in which women disciples are portrayed as serving throughout the New Testament and beyond. Following that, we will take up the question of women apostles.

## *DIAKONIA*: MORE THAN TABLE SERVICE

The Synoptic evangelists all say that the women had been serving or ministering (*diēkonoun*) to and with Jesus. The verb *diakonein* refers to a variety of different kinds of service. It occurs not only in the New Testament, but in secular Greek sources as well, where it has the meaning "to wait at table"[37] or "to provide or care for,"[38] often referring to the work of women. First-century Jewish historian Josephus uses *diakonein* in three senses: "to wait at table" (*Ant.* 6.52; 11.163); "to serve" with the meaning "to obey" (*Ant.* 9.25; 17.140); and "to render priestly service" (*Ant.* 7.365; 10.72).

In his comprehensive study of the term, John N. Collins shows that the basic meaning in non-Christian sources is to act as a "go-between," an agent who implements another person's intentions or desires.[39] In most instances in the New Testament, *diakonein* refers to ministry, and the agent on whose behalf one serves is Jesus and, ultimately, God. Throughout the New Testament, the verb *diakonein* and the noun *diakonia* refer to ministerial service of various kinds: financial ministry (Luke 8:3; Acts 11:29; 12:25), leadership (Luke 22:26), apostolic ministry (Acts 1:25), ministry of the table (Acts 6:2), ministry of the word (Acts 6:4), and the whole of Paul's ministerial service (Acts 20:24; 21:19).

Each of the Gospels employs the verb *diakonein* to refer both to Jesus's ministry and to that entrusted to his disciples. Jesus tells his followers he has come "not to be served [*diakonēthēnai*], but to serve [*diakonēsai*]" (Mark 10:45; similarly, Matt 20:28). In Luke's Gospel, the saying occurs in the Last Supper scene. Jesus speaks not only of his own service, but also instructs his disciples on their manner of servant leadership: "the greatest among you must become like the youngest, and the leader like one who serves [*ho diakonōn*]. For who is greater, the one who is at the table or the one who serves [*ho diakonōn*]? Is it not the one at the table? But I am among you as one who serves [*ho diakonōn*]" (22:26–27).[40] In the Gospel of John, shortly after he enters Jerusalem for the last time, Jesus declares, "Whoever serves [*diakonę̄*] me must follow me, and where I am, there will my servant [*diakonos*] be also" (12:26).

The only characters in the Gospels of whom the verb *diakonein* or the noun *diakonia* are used are female: Simon's mother-in-law, Martha, Mary Magdalene, Joanna, Susanna, and the other Galilean women who bankroll the mission and who witness Jesus's execution. In the Acts of the Apostles and in Paul's letters, Paul's ministry is called *diakonia*. In addition, there is an episode in Acts where *diakonia* involves widows. In his letter to the Romans, Paul speaks of Phoebe, *diakonos* of the church at Cenchreae. Finally, the author of 1 Timothy lists the qualifications for *diakonoi*, including female ministers. We will examine each of these references to ministering women in turn.

## *Simon's Mother-in-Law*[41]

In each of the Synoptic Gospels, the first use of the verb *diakonein* is in reference to Simon's mother-in-law (Mark 1:29–31 // Matt 8:14–15 // Luke 4:38–39), describing her response after Jesus heals her fever. The account is only two verses long, and there is little development of Simon's mother-in-law as a character in her own right. We do not know her name. She is identified only through her relationship to her son-in-law. She resides in his home, but the evangelists do not say why. Perhaps she is a widow with no children to care for her. There is no reference in the story to Peter's wife or to anyone else who lives in the house. Perhaps Simon's wife has died[42] and her mother has taken over responsibility for the household.

In none of the three accounts does Simon's mother-in-law speak, not to give voice to her suffering, nor to ask Jesus for healing. In Mark's and Luke's accounts, anonymous others intercede for her. All three versions end with her immediate healing and rising (*ēgerthē*, Matt 8:15; *anastasa*, Luke 4:39) or being raised (*ēgeiren*, Mark 1:31) followed by her serving (*diēkonei*). This final verse makes two important links with Jesus: the verbs used for her rising are the same used of Jesus's resurrection[43] and the verb for serving characterizes Jesus's own ministry.

Because *diakonein* is frequently used in the New Testament to mean ministerial service, several feminist scholars have proposed this meaning for Simon's mother-in-law's service.[44] Elaine Wainwright, for example, in analyzing Mark's version, suggests that the restoration of Simon's mother-in-law can be interpreted on two levels within the Markan community. At first, they might see her service as traditionally envisioned: domestic service to family and hospitality to guests. But with the imperfect form of the verb *diakonein* in this story and repeatedly hearing the end of the Gospel, where the Galilean women are said to have been ministering (15:41, again with *diakonein* in the imperfect), they might have come to see her as a ministering disciple, possibly among those at the foot of the cross or among those who, like the Twelve, were commissioned to heal others (Mark 6:12–13).[45]

Regarding Matthew 8:14–15, Wainwright notes several unique features in this version that point toward an underlying call story. She sees verbal and formal similarities between the call of Matthew (Matt 9:9) and the incident with Simon's mother-in-law. In both, Jesus takes the initiative,[46] a feature of call stories. By contrast, typically in healing stories, the person who is ill or someone who advocates for them approaches Jesus. Next, Jesus sees (*eiden*) Matthew and Simon's mother-in-law (8:14, 9:9). Also compare the call of the fishermen: "As Jesus passed along the Sea of Galilee, he saw (*eiden*) Simon and his brother Andrew casting a net into the sea" (Mark 1:16). The response in a call story is directly to Jesus, as when the fishermen leave their nets and follow him (*autǭ*, Matt 4:20, 22) and as Matthew leaves his tax booth and follows him (*autǭ*, 9:9). Simon's mother-in-law likewise directs her response to Jesus alone (*diēkonei autǭ*, 8:15). By contrast, in Mark's and Luke's versions, she serves "them" (*autois)*. Wainwright concludes that the original account was a call story with a healing motif, but in the final form, the healing story masks the call story.[47] By reading between the lines and connecting the dots, the possibility that Simon's mother-in-law was an important and well-known ministering disciple emerges.

Such a portrait does not come forth, however in Mark's and Luke's accounts, where Simon's mother-in-law is inside a house, apparently providing table service and hospitality to Simon and his companions. In contrast to Matthew 8:15, where Jesus alone is the object of her response (*autǭ*, "him"), in Mark 1:31 and Luke 4:39 the object of Simon's mother-in-law's service is plural (*autois*, "them"). Moreover, the context of her service is different from the outdoor settings in the crucifixion scene (Mark 15:40–41) and the episode where Mary Magdalene, Joanna, Susanna, and other women are traveling throughout the Galilee and ministering with Jesus (Luke 8:1–3). In the Markan and Lukan renditions of the story of Simon's mother-in-law, the context and language indicate table service and hospitality, whereas for Mary Magdalene and her companions at the crucifixion, ministerial service is indicated.[48]

It is important to appreciate that Simon's mother-in-law's ministry of table service and hospitality is every bit as essential and valuable as other forms of *diakonia*. In Luke 13:20–21 (similarly, Matt 13:33), Jesus tells a parable of a bakerwoman that illustrates how God's *basileia* is manifested through women's work. The everyday work of a woman baking bread has an impact far beyond the feeding of her family. In the parable, the woman is kneading three measures of flour—approximately fifty pounds! The amount evokes other biblical stories: three measures is what Sarah used when baking for the heavenly visitors (Gen 18:6);[49] Gideon uses the same amount when he prepares to receive an angel of God (Judg 6:19); and finally, Hannah uses "an ephah of flour," that is, about a bushel, for the offering she makes for the presentation of Samuel in the temple at Shiloh (1 Sam 1:24). In each instance, large-scale baking is associated with a divine manifestation. So, too, the work of the bakerwoman in the parable manifests God's *basileia*.[50] The huge amount of flour also points toward messianic fulfillment. Irenaeus says that in messianic times "a grain of wheat shall bring forth 10,000 ears, and every ear shall have 10,000 grains" (*Adv. Haer.* 5.33.3–4).

The woman's action of hiding the yeast in the flour[51] also evokes the divine way of concealing until the proper moment of revelation. Other passages in Luke using forms of the very *kryptō* illustrate this nuance. At 10:21, Jesus rejoices and thanks God: "because you have hidden [*apekrypsas*] these things from the wise and the intelligent and have revealed them to infants." When the Twelve do not understand about the passion, Jesus says it "was hidden [*kekrymmenon*] from them" (18:34). And when Jesus laments that Jerusalem has not recognized "the things that make for peace," he says, "But now they are hidden [*ekrybē*] from your eyes" (19:42). Just as in these instances, so in the parable, something about divine action is hidden until the proper time of full revelation. But God's *basileia* can already be partially experienced through the godly actions of a baker-woman who ensures that all have enough to eat. In this, she is bringing to fulfillment the hope Mary expresses in her Magnificat: that God who has "filled the hungry with good things" (1:53) will continue to do so, as does Jesus in the face of hungry crowds (Luke 9:10–17) and Woman Wisdom who invites all to her banquet (Prov 9:5).

Simon's mother-in-law embodies a manifestation of God through her ministry of feeding hungry people. Her story recalls the ministries of myriad women who not only baked but also presided over the blessing and distribution of bread at eucharistic gatherings in their homes.[52] This part of the Christian story is obscured when the evangelists focus on Jesus blessing, breaking, and distributing bread to hungry crowds (Mark 6:30–44 // Matt 14:13–21 // Luke 9:10–17) and to his disciples at the Last Supper (Mark 14:17–25 // Matt 26:20–29 // Luke 22:14–23). And when Jesus teaches his disciples to pray, it is a male "Father" who gives them their daily bread (Matt 6:9–15 // Luke 11:2–3).[53] Female bakers recede to the background as their work of providing bread becomes the domain of male leaders.

### *Mary Magdalene and Many Other Galilean Women*

Mary Magdalene and several female companions appear in each of the four Gospels. In all but Luke, they appear in the narrative for the first time at the crucifixion. Mark and Matthew indicate, however, that they have been there all along; they had been following Jesus (*ēkolouthoun autǭ*) and providing for or ministering with him (*diēkonoun autǭ*) (Mark 15:40–41 // Matt 27:55). The imperfect tense of the verbs points to ongoing repeated past actions. The one constant in every Gospel is Mary Magdalene. In the Synoptics she is always named first.

As the chart below shows, the names of her companions vary in the different Gospels, and several lists indicate that other unnamed women were also present.

| | Mark 15:40–41 | Matthew 27:56 | Luke (23:49)[54] | John (19:25)[55] |
|---|---|---|---|---|
| Crucifixion | Mary Magdalene<br>Mary the mother of James the younger and of Joses<br>Salome | Mary Magdalene<br>Mary the mother of James and Joseph<br>the mother of the sons of Zebedee | all his acquaintances, including the women who had followed him from Galilee | Jesus's mother<br>his mother's sister<br>Mary the wife of Clopas<br>Mary Magdalene |
| | Mark 15:47 | Matthew 27:61 | Luke 23:55 | John 19:38–42 |
| Burial | Mary Magdalene<br>Mary the mother of Joses | Mary Magdalene<br>the other Mary | The women who had come with him from Galilee | |
| | Mark 16:1 | Matthew 28:1 | Luke 24:10 | John 20:1 |
| Empty Tomb | Mary Magdalene<br>Mary the mother of James<br>Salome | Mary Magdalene<br>the other Mary | Mary Magdalene<br>Joanna<br>Mary the mother of James<br>the other women with them | Mary Magdalene |
| | Mark 16:9, 12 | Matthew 28:9 | Luke 24:13–35 | John 20:11–18, 19–23, 26–29 |
| Appearances of the Risen Christ | Mary Magdalene<br>Two unidentified followers | Mary Magdalene<br>the other Mary | Cleopas and his unnamed companion (his wife?) | Mary Magdalene<br>the disciples |

The only evangelist who specifies what kind of ministry Mary Magdalene and her companions are engaged in is Luke. Unlike the other Gospels, the women first appear in Luke when Jesus and the Twelve were preaching and evangelizing throughout the cities and villages of the Galilee (8:1). Along with them were "women who had been cured of evil spirits and infirmities: Mary, called Magdalene, from whom seven demons had gone out, and Joanna, the wife of Herod's steward Chuza, and Susanna, and many others, who provided for them [*diēkonoun*] out of their resources" (8:2–3).[56] Some commentators envision the "resources" of women as limited to domestic service such as making meals and clothes.[57] But the Greek expression *ek tōn hyparchontōn autais* makes it clear that the women's ministry is financial support. In Luke and Acts the noun *hyparchontōn* means possessions, property, money, or goods.[58] The women were not simply administering the common purse (see John 12:6, where that job belongs to Judas); rather, the monetary resources were their own, as indicated by the feminine plural pronoun *autais*, "their."[59] Some commentators presume women did not have money of their own in antiquity, but the Bible and other ancient sources give evidence to the contrary.[60]

It is not entirely clear, however, whether the women were themselves well-to-do or whether they were simply good at fundraising. In both the Gospel and Acts, Luke spotlights well-to-do supporters of the mission, such as Zacchaeus (Luke 19:1–10), Barnabas (Acts 4:36–37); a eunuch who oversees the treasury of the queen of the Ethiopians (Acts 8:27); Mary, the mother of John Mark, who had a house large enough to host the disciples in Jerusalem (Acts 12:12); Lydia, a dealer in luxury items (Acts 16:14);[61] prominent women in Thessalonica (Acts 17:4); influential Greek women and men in Beroea (Acts 17:12); Prisca and Aquila, who hosted Paul in Corinth (Acts 18:1–11) and who had the means to travel with Paul to Ephesus to establish a new mission base there (Acts 18:18–28). Most likely Luke intends us to view Mary Magdalene and the other women among these well-heeled supporters.

We remain curious as to the marital status of these women. Apart from Joanna, who is married to Chuza, there is no indication whether the other women were married, widowed, or single. It appears that they have control over how their money is spent, which would be unusual in a patriarchal context, but not unique. Inscriptional evidence from the first centuries CE attests that elite women provided patronage in civic and religious contexts.[62]

Beyond financial support, the women's ministry also includes faithful accompaniment of Jesus through the end of his fateful journey to Jerusalem. While the evangelists do not give them voice during Jesus's ministry, it is easy to imagine that in their interactions with him and the other disciples, Mary Magdalene and the other women offered their wisdom, visions, and hopes, helping to shape the mission as it unfolded. The final chapters of Matthew and John, along with many apocryphal works, portray these women as apostles, teachers, preachers, and evangelists. We will take up that part of their story below.

## *Martha and Mary*

Although there are two gospel episodes with Martha and Mary (Luke 10:38–42; John 11:1—12:8), the one that stands out for most Christians is Luke's story of the dispute brought to Jesus's attention when he comes to their home. For many, the account depicts the tension between action and contemplation in the life of a disciple. Mary, sitting at Jesus's feet and listening to him, has chosen the better part. What many miss is the object of Martha's worry: ***pollēn diakonian***, "much ministry" and that her sister has left her to do all the ministry, ***diakonein***, herself (10:40). There is no specification in the text what kind of ***diakonia*** preoccupies Martha. Rather than anxiety about food preparation, this vignette may well reflect the tensions in the Lukan church over women taking on roles in ministry that some Jesus followers thought proper only to men.[63] Luke sides with the latter, by triangulating the dispute and having Jesus make a definitive pronouncement.[64]

There are some interpreters who find this story good for women. They see in Jesus's affirmation of Mary the acceptance of women as disciples, finding a parallel between Mary and Paul, who was educated in the Law at the feet of Gamaliel (Acts 22:3).[65] They see Martha as overburdened, as are many women both ancient and contemporary, with domestic responsibilities from which Jesus can liberate them, giving them permission to engage in contemplation and study. Often there is an anti-Jewish twist, as some interpreters view Jesus as freeing women from what they think of as a restrictive and misogynistic Jewish world. Such interpreters wrongly assert that in ancient Judaism women were prohibited from studying Torah. They quote Rabbi Eliezer, who said, "If a man gives his daughter a knowledge of the Law it is as though he taught her lechery" (m. Sotah 3:4) and "Better to burn the Torah than place it in the mouth of a woman" (t. Sotah 21b). Such an approach is fraught with difficulties. First, these texts from the Mishnah date to approximately 175 years after Jesus's ministry. We do not know whether Rabbi Eliezer's opinion reflected the thinking of Jews of Jesus's day. What we do know from the writings of Philo of Alexandria, a contemporary of Jesus, is that there were women ascetics, the *Therapeutrides*, who dedicated their lives to the study of Torah (*Vit. Cont.* 68). There were also women who were leaders of synagogues, a position that would have required them to be educated in Torah.[66] Another difficulty is that these texts give only one side; in the same tractate of the Mishnah is Ben Azzai's opinion: "A man ought to give his daughter a knowledge of the Law" (m. Sotah 3:4). And m. Ned. 4:3 says that educating daughters as well as sons is a religious duty. Another serious problem is that this approach pits Jesus against Judaism, overlooking the fact that he was an observant Jew and his movement aimed at renewal *within* Judaism.[67] Finally, the way in which Mary and Martha are pitted against each other in a dualistic contrast is highly problematic. Mary's theological education is upheld at the expense of Martha's ministerial service. Nowhere else in Luke's Gospel does Jesus value contemplation or theological education over active ministerial service. It is always both/and. Discipleship in Luke consists in both hearing and acting on the word.[68] We also observe that both Martha (10:38) and Mary welcome the word. It is what they do with the word they hear that is the point of contention.

In the episode with the two sisters in John 11:1—12:8, there is an echo of some of the details from the Lukan depiction. But the message is very different. As in Luke, where the home is said to be Martha's (Luke 10:38), so in John, she acts as head of the household when she comes out from the village to welcome Jesus (John 11:21). Martha exhibits a well cultivated theological understanding and engages in an extended theological discussion with Jesus (11:21–27), which culminates in her declaration, "Yes, Lord, I believe that you are the Messiah, the Son of God, the one coming into the world" (11:27). The importance of Martha's pronouncement cannot be overstated when read in light of John 20:31, where the evangelist declares that the very purpose of writing this Gospel is "that you may come to believe that Jesus is the Messiah, the Son of God, and that through believing you may have life in his name." Moreover, Martha's christological confession takes on even more significance when we recall that in the Synoptic tradition, Peter makes this declaration (Matt 16:16; Mark 8:29; Luke 9:20).

As in Luke's Gospel, Martha is doing the serving, *diēkonei*, this time at the celebratory meal after Lazarus's resuscitation (John 12:2). In this context, Martha's serving at table indicates her prominence, much as Jesus's presiding at the Last Supper "as one who serves [*ho diakonōn*]" (Luke 22:27). As in Luke, Mary is at Jesus's feet, but this time she is anointing them, foreshadowing Jesus's own action in the following chapter (John 13:5–7). His washing of the disciples' feet is the model for them to emulate: self-emptying love to the death for their friends (13:15). In the Fourth Gospel, there is no conflict between Martha and Mary. Both dialogue with Jesus in a way that reflects theological astuteness. Both put their discipleship into practice through selfless ministerial service.

### Phoebe

The only person in the New Testament who bears the title *diakonos* is Phoebe, for whom Paul writes a recommendation in the last chapter of his letter to the Romans (16:1–2).[69] While some translations render *diakonos* as "deaconess," the Greek noun is, in fact, both masculine and feminine; there is no basis for making a distinction between Phoebe and male deacons. *Diakonos* is better translated as "minister,"[70] as there were no fixed job descriptions or ordination rituals for "deacons" in Paul's day. What we can glean about the work done by "deacons" comes from the ways in which the verb *diakonein* and the noun *diakonia* are used in the Gospels and Acts (see above, pp. 32–34). Phoebe could have been engaged in any or all of the diaconal ministries of preaching, teaching, evangelizing, and presiding over the eucharistic gatherings. She likely had financial resources that she used for the support of the community. There was an apostolic dimension to her ministry, as Romans 16 depicts her in the role of ambassador of Paul to Rome. In addition to being the carrier of the letter, Phoebe may also have been the one who read it aloud to the various house churches in Rome. Perhaps Paul discussed with her how to respond to any questions that may have arisen from the letter.[71]

Another word used of Phoebe in Romans 16:2, *prostatis*, fills in more of the picture of her ministry as a leader. This noun is translated in various ways: "helper" (RSV), "good friend" (NEB), "a great help" (NIV), "benefactor" (NRSV, NABRE). All these renderings fall short. When used in secular Greek literature, *prostatis* connotes "leader" or "ruler" in a political sense. In the Roman period, it was used for patrons or benefactors, that is, women and men who provided funds and protection and used their political influence for those under their patronage. However, "patron" does not capture all that Romans 16:2 implies; she did not only provide funds for the community at Cenchreae; the context indicates that her role as leader and administrator was far greater. Startlingly, Paul acknowledges her leadership not only "of many" but even of himself as well (Rom 16:2)! It is possible that she had more influence over the community at Cenchreae than Paul did, since he was there only temporarily.[72]

## *Ministering Widows*

One final occurrence of *diakonia* and *diakonein* in connection with women occurs in Acts, when "the Hellenists complained against the Hebrews because their widows were being neglected in the daily distribution [*diakonia*] of food" (Acts 6:1). It is not at all clear what was the nature of the problem between the Greek speakers and the Hebrew speakers in the community in Jerusalem. The conflict involved *diakonia*, but what kind of ministry is not specified (see above, pp. 32–34, for the various kinds of ministries connoted by *diakonia*). The translators of the NRSV have made a presumption by rendering *diakonia kathēmerinę̄* as "daily distribution of food." The specification "of food" is not in the Greek text. Most commentators imagine widows as needy and dependent and thus presume that they were the recipients of the ministry. Indeed, the admonition to care for widows, orphans, and aliens is often repeated in the Bible (e.g., Deut 26:12; James 1:27). But in Luke and Acts, most widows are performing ministry, not receiving it. Consider Anna prophesying in the temple (Luke 2:36–38), the widow who gives her whole livelihood/life to the temple (Luke 21:1–4), Dorcas, likely a widow, who houses other ministering widows (Acts 9:36–43). In addition, it is likely that among the Galilean women who ministered financially (Luke 8:3), some would have been widows (except for Joanna, nothing is said about the marital status of Mary Magdalene, Susanna, and the other Galilean women). Simon's mother-in-law (Luke 4:38–39) may also have been a widow, which could explain why she is living with her son-in-law. Martha and/or Mary may have been widows (Luke 10:38–42).[73]

With the prominence of ministering widows in Luke and Acts, it may well have been the case that the conflict in Acts 6 centers on widows who were being overlooked by the leaders of the community when ministerial assignments were given. Elisabeth Schüssler Fiorenza advances that the tensions were around the role and participation of women at the eucharistic meal: the Hellenist widows were not being assigned their turn in the table service.[74] This interpretation is supported by the fact that table sharing was said to take place daily (Acts 2:46). Eucharistic table ministry included preparation of the meal, purchase and distribution of food, serving food during the meal, and cleaning up afterward. It is possible that the Hellenist women were more accustomed to participating in festive meals with symposia (see more on this below) and may have taken for granted that they would actively participate in the ministerial roles at the eucharistic meals in Christian house churches, whereas such practices proved more problematic for the Hebrews.

Whatever was the problem, the resolution comes from the Twelve: they appoint seven Hellenist men to minister at the table (*diakonein trapezais*, 6:2),[75] while they devote themselves to ministry of the word (*diakonia tou logou*, 6:4). This dichotomy between the two kinds of ministry does not hold up in the rest of the narrative. In the very next episodes in Acts, Stephen, one of those chosen for table ministry (6:5), is depicted as debating with wisdom and spirit (6:8–15) and then delivering a lengthy speech (7:2–53). Philip, another who was supposed to exercise table ministry (Acts 6:5), is next shown going from place to place proclaiming the word (Acts 8:4, 40) and interpreting a text from Isaiah for an Ethiopian eunuch (8:26–39). In his next appearance in Acts 21:8, he is called "Philip the evangelist" and four of his daughters have the gift of prophecy (21:9), a ministry of the word that he may have helped cultivate in them. No mention is made of Philip serving at table.

The way in which the decision was made in Acts 6 is disturbing to modern feminists. The problem involves widows, but they are not involved in arriving at the resolution. The two groups of widows are not invited to give their sides of the story as are Peter and Paul in Acts 15. There is no consultation, discussion, or weighing of different solutions. There is no invocation of the Spirit in the decision-making.[76] The decision to choose men from among their own ranks is made unilaterally by the Twelve and is then said to have pleased the whole community (6:5). We wonder. If the widows were being bypassed in the daily assignment of ministries, would not the solution proposed by the Twelve only have exacerbated the conflict, making the women even more invisible?

We can see in this episode that Luke is more firmly cementing his portrait of leadership as belonging to males in the early communities of Jesus's followers. Although there are clearly women as well as men in the community of disciples—recall that Tabitha is explicitly called a disciple in Acts 9:36—and women are clearly exercising leadership in the early Christian communities, Luke is intent on assigning leadership only to male followers.[77]

## *Qualities of Ministers*

In the First Letter to Timothy, there is a list of qualities that are desired for "deacons":

> [8]Deacons likewise must be serious, not double-tongued, not indulging in much wine, not greedy for money; [9]they must hold fast to the mystery of the faith with a clear conscience. [10]And let them first be tested; then, if they prove themselves blameless, let them serve as deacons. [11]Women likewise must be serious, not slanderers, but temperate, faithful in all things. [12]Let deacons be married only once, and let them manage their children and their households well; [13]for those who serve well as deacons gain a good standing for themselves and great boldness in the faith that is in Christ Jesus. (1 Tim 3:8–13)

It is not clear whether the women in verse 11 are (1) generic women; (2) wives of male deacons; (3) a separate group of women ministers; (4) women deacons ministering jointly with men deacons. The Greek word *gynaikas* allows for any of these meanings. The first possibility, that this is a reference to women in the congregation as a whole, with verse 11 serving as a kind of addendum to the discussion of women's behavior and dress in 2:9–10, is most unlikely, given that the context of 3:1–13 is a discussion of various modes of ministerial service. In favor of the second interpretation, that the reference is to wives of male deacons, is that the author takes a restrictive stance toward women's ministerial leadership elsewhere in the letter.[78] That the reference is to a separate group of women deacons is supported by the use of the word *likewise*, which seems to introduce a new group, parallel to male deacons. It is also notable that several early church fathers interpreted 1 Timothy 3:11 as referring to women appointed to the office of deacon.[79]

More recently, the fourth option has been gaining favor: the content and structure of the passage point toward women who are ministering along with men as deacons.[80] Jennifer Steifel advances that the *diakonoi* addressed in verse 8 be read as inclusive of women and men deacons. Verse 11 addresses women deacons within the order of deacons and male deacons, as heads of households, are addressed in verse 12.[81] Although not completely conclusive, the evidence for this fourth interpretation from linguistic and literary analysis is strong.[82]

While agreeing with Steifel's overall interpretation, I would like to suggest that the qualities of a good household manager listed in verse 12 could also be read as applying to women. Though the *paterfamilias* was certainly considered the head of the household in a patriarchal world, household management was the domain of women.[83] It is easy to imagine that managing their households well was a factor in the rise to leadership of those women who are featured in the New Testament as heads of house churches: Nympha (Col 4:15), Lydia (Acts 16:14, 40), Mary, the mother of John Mark (Acts 12:12), Prisca (Rom 16:5), and Martha (Luke 10:38; John 11:1—12:8).

Even if the author of 1 Timothy was not speaking of female deacons in 3:11, they most certainly existed in the early church. Inscriptions and documents show that they became quite prominent in some parts of the early church and persisted into the twelfth century. The *Didascalia Apostolorum* (third-fourth century) prescribes the necessity for women deacons to minister to other women and children, while also asserting,

> We affirm that the service of a woman, a Deaconess is necessary and obligatory, because even our Lord and Saviour was served by the hand of women deaconesses, who were Mary the Magdalene and Mary of James, the mother of Joses, and the mother of Zebedee's children, with other women.[84]

The ongoing legacy of Deacon Phoebe (Rom 16:1–2) is attested by a tombstone dating to the fourth century, found on the Mount of Olives in 1903, inscribed, "Here lies the minister and bride of Christ, Sofia the deacon [*diakonos*], the second Phoebe." The contemporary movement toward restoring women to the diaconate has good biblical and historical basis.[85]

In this section we have seen that *diakonia* refers to many kinds of ministries and that a whole host of women in the New Testament are depicted performing these services. Like Woman Wisdom, many prepared and presided over table gatherings; others preached, evangelized, taught, and financed the mission, using their myriad gifts to feed the hungers of hurting people.

## WOMEN APOSTLES

In the previous section, we examined the occurrences of *diakonia*, *diakonein*, and *diakonos* to explore the ways that women were exercising ministry in the early communities of Jesus followers. While Christians may be cognizant of women's participation in the early Jesus movement, many still think that those entrusted with apostolic ministry were a special group that consisted only of twelve men called and sent by Jesus (Mark 3:13–19; 6:7–13; Matt 10:1–16; Luke 6:12–16; 9:1–6). The word *apostolos*, "apostle," means "one sent." In the Synoptic narratives of the calling and sending of the Twelve, who are explicitly named "apostles" (Mark 3:14; 6:30; Matt 10:2; Luke 6:13; 9:10), what characterizes them is that they are chosen and called by Jesus to be with him and then they are sent out to preach, heal, and exorcise demons.

The notion that only twelve men were appointed to apostolic ministry unravels when we look more closely at the New Testament evidence. First is the question: which twelve? There are four lists of the Twelve (Mark 3:16–19; Matt 10:2–4; Luke 6:14–16; Acts 1:13) and they do not agree. The memory that there were "twelve" in number is stronger than the recollection of who they were. A further question arises as to whether there was actually an identifiable historical group known as "the Twelve."[86] Whichever way one answers, twelve is a symbolic number: twelve was the number of tribes of Israel. The twelve called by Jesus symbolizes a reconstituted full number of God's people. Rather than read the twelve as an exclusive group given a unique mission, we may read them as symbolic for what is entrusted to the whole of God's people in the Jesus movement. All are called to be "missionary disciples," as Pope Francis has alerted us.

It is also important to note that the New Testament speaks of many more than twelve apostles. In Luke's Gospel, in addition to the sending of the Twelve, there is an identical sending of a further seventy[87] apostles in pairs. While some scholars envision women among these pairs, it is unlikely that Luke wanted to convey that, given his proclivity to restrict leadership to males. See, for example, Acts 1:25, where Luke's list of qualifications for choosing Judas's replacement for "the ministry of apostleship" (*tēs diakonias tautēs kai apostolēs*) includes that he be "one of the men [*andrōn*][88] who have accompanied us during all the time that the Lord Jesus went in and out among us, beginning from the baptism of John until the day when he was taken up from us" (Acts 1:21–22). In Paul's letters, there are numerous other apostles named, prime among them Paul himself. Paul repeatedly calls himself an apostle[89] and uses the term of a number of other coworkers: Apollos (1 Cor 4:6, 9), Barnabas (1 Cor 9:5–6),[90] Epaphroditus (Phil

2:25), Sylvanus and Timothy (1 Thess 1:1 with 2:7), James (Gal 1:19), and Andronicus and Junia (Rom 16:7). This last apostle is a woman. We will return to her shortly. In addition to those explicitly named apostles, there are several women who are portrayed as apostles in the Gospels and in many extracanonical traditions. We look now at these in more detail.

### *Junia, Prominent among the Apostles*

Junia is the only woman in the New Testament explicitly named an apostle. She appears among those to whom Paul sends greetings in the final chapter of his letter to the Romans. He says, "Greet Andronicus and Junia, my relatives who were in prison with me; they are prominent among the apostles, and they were in Christ before I was" (Rom 16:7). There are many unanswered questions that this short verse raises. What is the relationship between Andronicus and Junia? Husband and wife? Brother and sister? Cousins? Unrelated companions? How are they related to Paul? Where and when were they imprisoned together? What made them so prominent?[91]

One further question is whether Junia was a woman or a man. The name in the Greek text is *Iounian* (in the accusative case) and could be either masculine (Junias) or feminine (Junia).[92] The evidence is overwhelmingly in support of Junia, a woman. The female name is well attested in Latin and Greek inscriptions and ancient literature, whereas the masculine name Junias has yet to be found. Most importantly, all early commentators on the Letter to the Romans understood the reference to be to a woman. John Chrysostom (ca. 347–407), for example, says, "Indeed, how great the wisdom of this woman must have been that she was even deemed worthy of the title of apostle."[93] Others who interpreted *Iounian* to be a woman include Origen of Alexandria (ca. 185–253/54), Jerome (340/50–419/20), Hatto of Vercelli (924–961), Theophylact (1050–1108), and Peter Abelard (1079–1142).[94] It was not until the thirteenth century that commentators began to take the name as masculine, beginning with Aegidius of Rome (1245–1316). They presumed that a woman could not be an apostle, therefore the name had to be that of a man.[95]

### *Photina, an Enlightened Samaritan Apostle*

Although the biblical text does not name her "apostle," the Samaritan woman who encounters Jesus at a well and then brings her townspeople to faith in him (John 4:4–42), is so designated by several early church fathers. Origen (185–ca. 251), for example, referred to her as an apostle and evangelist: "Christ sends the woman as an apostle to the inhabitants of the city because his words have inflamed this woman."[96] When interpreters allow sexism, xenophobia, and fascination with sexual sins to fog their vision, they miss what Origen and others saw so clearly. In this Gospel, there is no calling or sending of the Twelve. There are two references to the Twelve at the end of the Bread of Life discourse (6:67, 70) as well as the identification of Judas as "one of the twelve" (6:71) and later Thomas (20:24). They are not said to be apostles; the only time the noun *apostolos* appears in this Gospel is in the Last Supper scene, where Jesus says to his disciples, "Very truly, I tell you, servants [*apostolos*] are not greater than their master, nor are messengers greater than the one who sent them" (13:16). The verb *apostellein* ("to send"), however, appears frequently in the Fourth Gospel, often referring to Jesus having been sent by the Father. In his final prayer, Jesus speaks of all his disciples[97] as apostles: "As you have sent [*apesteilas*] me into the world, so I have sent [*apesteila*] them into the world" (17:18).

In this Gospel, the one who embodies apostleship is the woman from Samaria. Through her testimony (*dia ton logon tēs gynaikos martyrousēs*, lit. "through the word of the witnessing woman"), she brings many in her city to believe in Jesus and to seek to abide with him (4:40). In the opening verses of the Gospel, Jesus himself is the Word, *logos*; here, through her word, *logos*, the woman accomplishes the very goal of this Gospel: "that you may come to believe that Jesus is the Messiah, the Son of God, and that through believing you may have life in his name" (20:31). The believing Samaritans want to have Jesus stay with (*menein*) them (4:40), pointing ahead to the final discourse, where Jesus entreats his disciples to abide (*menein*) in him as he in them (15:1–11).

Some readers of this Gospel fail to see the woman as an apostle, having the false impression that she is a sinner, something that is absent from the text. Some interpret her coming to the well at noon as an effort to avoid encounter with others, who would shun her for her sinfulness. This line of reasoning misses the deep theological symbolism of light and darkness that is so prominent in this Gospel.[98] The evangelist has set up a strong contrast between Nicodemus in the previous chapter, who comes to Jesus at night, and this woman who comes at the brightest part of the day. Nicodemus is unable to come to belief in Jesus;[99] the woman comes to full faith, perceiving Jesus as Messiah (4:25) and leading others to believe in him as Savior of the world (4:42). Narratively, it does not make sense to think of the woman as a shunned sinner. If that were the case, how is it that the people in her city so readily listen to her and believe her word?

Another part of the episode that calls the attention of many readers away from the woman's apostolic role is the dialogue about the five husbands (4:16–19). Numerous commentators interpret her serial marriages and her current unmarried liaison as indications of her sinfulness and immoral way of life.[100] What they miss is that the whole chapter is a highly theological and symbolic dialogue, and the exchange about the husbands needs to be read in that way as well. The woman is a representative character,[101] embodying all of Samaria, whom Jesus is inviting into intimate (using a marital metaphor) relationship with the God of Israel. Reading symbolically, the five husbands can be taken as an allusion to the five false gods of the Assyrians that Samaria adopted when they were conquered by them (2 Kgs 17:13–34).[102] In Hebrew, *ba'al* means both "husband"

and "Lord," or "God." Jesus's statement that the one she has now is not her "husband," can be interpreted as him saying that Samaria is not espoused to the God of Israel, as they should be. The prophets often used the metaphor of YHWH as the faithful husband and Israel as the bride who strays (see especially Hosea 2)—a metaphor that has received much feminist critique! The woman catches this allusion, responding, "I see that you are a prophet" (4:19). Reading 4:16–19 this way builds on the marital theme that emerges in the preceding chapters with the wedding feast at Cana (2:1–12) and John the Baptist's declaration that he is the best man, not the bridegroom (3:27–30). Moreover, the setting at a well, where a man and a woman meet, evokes stories of patriarchs or their servants who meet their future wives at a well, such as Isaac and Rebekah (Gen 24:10–61), Jacob and Rachel (Gen 29:1–20), Moses and Zipporah (Exod 2:16–22).

Luise Schottroff takes a different approach, elaborating the reasons why a woman might have consecutive marriages—not because she is immoral, but rather because of the vulnerable and unsustainable position of being a single, divorced, or widowed woman in a patriarchal world. Serial marriages were common, and this woman had to marry repeatedly for economic and social reasons. After five marriages, the woman is now in a situation of sexual exploitation; that is, the man she is living with currently does not even offer her the security of a marriage contract. Her encounter with Jesus emboldens her to choose to leave this degrading situation. By becoming part of the Jesus movement, she obtains a new family and household in which she can survive as an independent woman. She is transformed into an apostolic messenger, offering others the water of life.[103]

Some interpreters do not see the Samaritan woman as an apostle who comes to full faith; they read her as still questioning when she says, "He cannot be the Messiah, can he?" (4:29).[104] In addition, they see Jesus's own word, not the woman's, that converts her townspeople: "And many more believed because of his word. They said to the woman, 'It is no longer because of what you said that we believe, for we have heard for ourselves, and we know that this is truly the Savior of the world'" (4:41–42). The woman's query, however, is better read as a rhetorical question, "Is this not the Christ?" (4:29), a literary device that invites the villagers as well as the contemporary reader to enter into their own journey of coming to faith in Jesus.[105] Moreover, this chapter follows a pattern that is consistent in the Fourth Gospel: those who come to believe in Jesus bring others to him. In the opening chapter, John the Baptist directs two of his disciples to Jesus and they follow him (1:35–39). One of them is Andrew, who then brings his brother Simon Peter to Jesus, using words like those of the Samaritan woman, "We have found the Messiah!" (1:40–42). At the end of the Gospel, Mary Magdalene is sent to bring her brothers and sisters to belief in Jesus as risen (20:17). In like fashion, the Samaritan woman, who has come to belief, shares the good news with others and is a conduit of faith for them.

In Eastern tradition, the Samaritan woman is given the name Photina, "Enlightened One," and she is held in high regard. There are numerous legends about her, filling in the blanks of what happened after she met Jesus. Most of them elaborate on her continued preaching of the good news. One legend tells of her living and preaching in Carthage. Another tells of the effectiveness of her preaching while imprisoned: she converted Nero's daughter, Domnina. As the story goes, she was then flayed alive and thrown down a well, a bitter irony in light of the fact that it was at a well that she encountered and came to faith in Jesus. Another tradition is that her head was preserved in Rome in the Church of St. Paul Outside the Walls, which led Cardinal Cesare Baronius (1538–1607) to include her in the Roman martyrology. Preserving the insight of Origen, a Byzantine prayer recognizes Photina not only as a martyr, but as "equal to the apostles":

> Illuminated by the Holy Spirit, All-Glorious One,
> from Christ the Saviour you drank the water of
> salvation.
> With open hand you give it to those who thirst.
> Great-Martyr Photina, Equal-to-the-Apostles,
> pray to Christ for the salvation of our souls.[106]

In the Greek calendar, Photina is commemorated on February 26.

## *Mary Magdalene: Apostle to Other Apostles*

We have examined the ways in which Mary Magdalene and the other Galilean women ministered with their financial resources and accompanied Jesus during his ministry in the Galilee, culminating in their faithfully following him to Jerusalem and witnessing his execution. Each of the four Gospels attests to the women witnesses and to their being the first to be entrusted with the good news at the empty tomb. However, each evangelist tells the story differently, some making the women apostles, others downplaying their role as preachers of the good news.

### *The Gospel of Mark*

In the Gospel of Mark, Mary Magdalene, Mary the mother of James,[107] and Salome[108] bring spices to the tomb to anoint the body (something that the woman in 14:3–9 has already done!). Inside the tomb, they encounter a young man dressed in white and they are amazed (*exethambēthēsan*, 16:5). The young man exhorts them not to be amazed and tells them Jesus has risen. He then commissions them, "Go, tell his disciples and Peter that he is going ahead of you to Galilee; there you will see him, just as he told you" (16:7). The scene ends abruptly: "So they went out and fled from the tomb, for terror and amazement [*tromos kai ekstasis*] had seized them; and they said nothing to anyone, for they were afraid" (16:8).

Since earliest times, people have struggled with this unsatisfactory ending in which the women do not fulfill their apostolic mission. As early as the second century, scribes added endings that would clarify and reassure.[109] Having previously been portrayed as such faithful followers, the women's failure is startling. They had kept vigil at the cross all day (15:40) from the time of Jesus's crucifixion at nine o'clock in the morning (15:25), through the darkness of noon (15:33) and his death around three in the afternoon (15:33, 37). They are still there when evening comes and Joseph of Arimathea asks to remove the body (15:42–43). They are still faithfully keeping watch[110] when Joseph lays him in the tomb (15:47).

A closer look at the words used of the women's reaction and how Mark uses those words elsewhere in the Gospel sheds light on how to understand 16:8. This is not the first time that disciples react with fear to amazing occurrences. In 4:41 Jesus's followers "fear a great fear" (*ephobēthēsan phobon megan*) after Jesus calmed the storm, perhaps suggesting more "awe" or "amazement," even epiphany, rather than fright. Likewise, when Jesus walks on the water, the disciples are terrified (*etarachthēsan*) and he urges them once again, "do not be afraid" (6:50; as also 4:40). In 16:8, might this instance also be one where the reaction is more awe than fright? The word used to describe the women's reaction in 16:5, *exethambēthēsan*, is also used to describe Jesus's emotions in Gethsemane as he confronts his imminent death (14:33). In that instance, it clearly connotes terror. The same verb is used of the crowd's response to Jesus as he comes down from the mountain where he had been transfigured, rendered by the NRSV as "overcome with awe" (9:15). There, the crowds are not afraid of him but run forward to greet Jesus. So too, in 16:5, the women's response is awe in the presence of something inexplicable that is divinely wrought. It is holy awe at the power and presence of God. Silence (16:8) is the appropriate response to such an experience.

The women's flight from the tomb (16:8) has a resonance with the flight of the male followers from Gethsemane (14:50). One way to understand the final verse is that it accords with a theme echoed throughout the Gospel: all followers fail, yet they endure as disciples. Another explanation is that Mark is not recounting a historical failure on the part of the women—the good news was, after all, proclaimed. Rather, this is a rhetorical strategy by which Mark invites the hearers of the Gospel to tell what the women did not. We finish the story with our lives—both through proclamation of and living the gospel.[111]

## *The Gospel of Matthew*

Matthew's account of the scene at the tomb follows the basic contours of Mark's, but with some significant differences. In this Gospel, the women's reaction is characterized as "fear and great joy" (*phobou kai karos megalēs*, 28:8), and they do exactly as the angel instructed: they leave the tomb quickly and run to tell the disciples (28:8). Also different from Mark is that Jesus meets the women and greets them. They then come to him, take hold of his feet, and worship him (28:9). That they can seize his feet attests to the reality and tangibility of the risen Jesus. He is not a ghost or a spirit. Nor is he simply present to them in memory. Their worship is the appropriate response to a manifestation of the divine.[112] Jesus repeats the angel's admonition not to fear (28:5, 10) and reiterates the commission himself, directing the women to go tell the other disciples to go to Galilee, where they will see him (28:10).

The women then fade from view as attention shifts to the guards and the chief priests as they concoct a plan to spread the word that the disciples stole the body in the night while the guards slept (28:11–15). That the women faithfully fulfilled the command is implied when they are said to go forth just after Jesus sends them, "While they were going..." (28:11). The other disciples evidently believe them and do as they say: "Now the eleven disciples went to Galilee, to the mountain to which Jesus directed them" (28:16), and like the women, they too worshiped him (*prosekynesan*, 28:17) when they saw him. The Gospel concludes with Jesus commissioning the eleven disciples, presumably the twelve men named in 10:2–4 less Judas Iscariot. Having been sent previously only to "the lost sheep of the house of Israel" to "proclaim the good news... cure the sick, raise the dead, cleanse the lepers, cast out demons" (10:6–8), Jesus now sends them to "make disciples of all nations" (28:19). The women who were first to see the risen Christ and to have faithfully conveyed the good news to the others drop out of view as the final commissioning is only to the eleven (male) disciples.

### *The Gospel of Luke*

In the Gospel of Luke, the women's reaction moves from perplexity (*aporeisthai*, 24:4) at finding the tomb empty to terror (*emphobōn*) and homage (*klinousōn ta prosōpa autōn eis tēn gēn*, "bowed their faces to the ground") when they encounter the two men in dazzling clothes inside the tomb (24:5). The heavenly figures ask, "Why do you look for the living among the dead?" before they declare, as in Mark and Matthew, "He is not here, but has risen" (Luke 24:5; cf. Mark 16:6; Matt 28:6). Their question invites the hearer of the Gospel herself to wrestle with this profound question. Unique to Luke is the angels' instruction: "Remember how he told you, while he was still in Galilee, that the Son of Man must be handed over to sinners, and be crucified, and on the third day rise again" (24:6–7). And they do (24:8).

The exhortation to remember Jesus's word (24:6) calls to mind various statements earlier in the Gospel about hearing the word and taking care of it.[113] The Galilean women are like Mary, who kept the word (*rhēmata*) in her heart (2:19, 51). They are the good soil who have heard the word and "hold it fast in an honest and good heart, and bear fruit with patient endurance" (8:15). Remembering means far more than simple recall. In the Old Testament, admonitions to remember the covenant always imply action. For example, when

God instructs Moses to have the Israelites make fringes on the corners of their garments, it is so they will remember and keep all the commandments (Num 15:39).[114] This kind of response is patterned on divine remembrance, which results in saving action.[115] In the opening chapter of Luke, Mary and Zechariah both sing of God's remembrance that is manifest in saving deeds (1:54, 72). Throughout the Gospel, Jesus embodies this divine saving remembrance in his actions, something that the criminal crucified alongside Jesus recognizes when he pleads, "Jesus, remember me when you come into your kingdom" (23:42). Unique among the Gospels[116] is Jesus's instruction to his disciples at the Last Supper, "Do this in remembrance [*anamnēsin*] of me" (22:19). He is asking the disciples to do more than simply bring him to mind as they break bread together; they are to make him present through all their merciful actions. All these instances in which remembering is featured in Luke help to flesh out the meaning of the women's remembering at the empty tomb. Remembering Jesus's words signifies not only that they were present when he spoke to the disciples in Galilee, but also that they faithfully continue to put into action divine liberating mercy.[117]

Mary Magdalene and her companions tell "all this to the eleven and to all the rest" (Luke 24:9). Luke describes the reception of their proclamation this way: "But these words seemed to them an idle tale [*lēros*], and they did not believe them" (24:11). We are left with an ambiguous message. One way to read this scene is that women's words are idle talk, ravings, nonsense, humbug, devoid of anything worthwhile.[118] For Luke, women have "chosen the better part" when they remain silent recipients of the word (as Mary in 10:38–42). It is for the male apostles to do the preaching and evangelizing. Accordingly, the risen Christ in Luke does not directly commission the women to proclaim the good news. Nor does he appear to them. For Luke, Peter is the first to have seen the Risen One (24:34), and he and Paul and the male apostles take center stage in the preaching mission in Acts. The message to a woman reader of Luke and Acts is that if she dares to speak, she will never be believed nor be credited with faithful and true witness.[119]

Another way to read the empty tomb scene in Luke is to see it within the wider context of the whole Gospel. With Luke's emphasis throughout on hearing and acting on the word, there is no need for a special commission to proclaim the good news. The women's spontaneous annunciation is the proper response of faithful disciples (see comments above on Hearing and Acting on the Word). Moreover, the verb *elegon*, "told" (24:10), is in the imperfect tense, indicating repeated telling. Mary Magdalene and her companions were not one-time messengers; they continued to proclaim the word as faithful witnesses.[120] The next scene affirms their reliability as witnesses, where Cleopas and his companion[121] repeat their message and report that it has been verified: "Some of those who were with us went to the tomb and found it just as the women had said; but they did not see him" (24:24). From this perspective, those who refuse to believe (24:11) are made to look foolish.

In the Fourth Gospel, Mary Magdalene comes to the tomb alone, representing the whole community of beloved disciples.[122] It is still dark when she arrives, signaling to the reader that she is about to embark on a further journey to the light of full faith. As in so many Johannine scenes, the process of coming to the light is a gradual one. Mary begins in sorrow and confusion, reporting to Peter and the disciple whom Jesus loved[123] that "they have taken the Lord out of the tomb, and we do not know where they have laid him" (20:2). The question "where" is central throughout the Gospel—where Jesus is from, where he is going, where he is to be found (e.g., John 1:38; 7:34, 36; 8:14, 21–22; 14:3–4; 17:24). In John 20:3–18, the answer comes in two parts.[124] First, when Peter and the other disciple run to the tomb and see only the linen wrappings and not the body, we come to understand that Jesus has returned to God to take up the glory he had before (see 17:5). These two disciples do not yet understand that Jesus has been raised and they simply return home (20:9–10).

The second part of the answer comes in 20:11–18 in Mary Magdalene's encounters with the risen Christ. Different from the Synoptic accounts, the angels do not tell Mary he has been raised, nor do they send her to tell the others; this will be conveyed to her directly by Jesus himself. After mistaking him for a gardener[125] and then recognizing him when he speaks her name,[126] she calls him, "Rabbouni," that is, "my Teacher." He then instructs her not to cling to the way she knew him previously, as he has ascended to the Father (20:17).[127] He commissions her to go to his brothers and sisters, the community of beloved disciples, to tell them that where he is to be found now is in their midst (20:17).[128] She faithfully announces, "'I have seen the Lord'; and she told them that he had said these things to her" (20:18).[129] In this Gospel there is no hint that the others did not believe her.[130]

In summary, we see diverse interpretations of Mary Magdalene and her companions when it comes to their portrayal as apostles of the good news. In Matthew and John, they are the first to see the risen Christ and are directly commissioned by him to tell the others, which they do. In Luke, Peter displaces the women as first to see the Risen One (24:34). Similarly, in Paul's list of all those to whom the risen Christ appeared, Cephas (the Aramaic name for Peter) heads the list, followed by the Twelve, then "more than five hundred brothers and sisters at one time," then James, then all the apostles, and lastly, Paul himself (1 Cor 15:5–8). He makes no mention of Mary Magdalene and her companions.

## *Ongoing Traditions*

Beyond the Gospels, there are numerous traditions, legends, and artistic works that continue to preserve the memory of Mary Magdalene as an apostle. Apocryphal works, such as *The Gospel of Mary*, capture the tensions between Mary and the male apostles. In this second-century Gospel, Mary recounts the visions and revelations she has received from Christ. Peter declares he cannot believe the Savior would reveal himself to a woman rather than to the men. Levi finally comes to Mary's defense and persuades the men to go off and preach as Mary had urged them to do.[131] One notable commentary from Hippolytus of Rome, writing in the early third century, says that the women who met the risen Christ "were made apostles to the apostles, having been sent by Christ."[132] Later legends tell of Mary going to southern France to preach and to baptize. In some of them, Martha accompanies her, a tradition preserved in stained glass windows from the late thirteenth century in the cathedral at Semur in Burgundy. In our own day, Pope Francis elevated the memorial of Mary Magdalene on July 22 to a feast day in the Catholic Church's liturgical calendar. Mass on that day now also includes a preface titled "Apostle of the apostles."

## *Towering Mary*

The high regard in which Mary was held in Christian tradition may be seen in the epithet attached to her: Magdalene. Most commonly, ***hē magdalēnē*** is thought to mean that Mary was from Magdala, a town on the northwest shore of the Sea of Galilee. The name Magdala derives from the Hebrew word ***migdal***, "tower," and has been thought to refer to a tower in which fish was smoked, a famous export of this fishing village.[133] Many have thought that this is the same village referred to in rabbinic literature as Migdal Nunya, "the Tower of Fish." A difficulty with this interpretation is that in the first century the town was called Tarichaea, not Magdala. Moreover, ancient authors such as Origen, Eusebius of

Caesarea, and Jerome understood "Magdalene" to refer to Mary's character rather than her hometown. Much as Simon was dubbed "Peter," "Rock," so Mary was recognized as "Towering," "Great," "Magnificent," for her faith and ministry.[134]

There is, however, another side to traditions about Mary Magdalene. Despite there being no evidence whatsoever in the Gospels to support them, myths, legends, and artwork abound depicting Mary as a repentant prostitute.[135] Unlike Peter, who declares his sinfulness when Jesus calls him to be a disciple (Luke 5:1–11), no such canonical story exists about Mary. Fueling the misperceptions of Mary Magdalene is that she is often confused with other Marys and unnamed women in the Gospels: Mary of Bethany (John 12:1–8); the unnamed woman who anoints Jesus (Mark 14:3–10; Matt 26:6–13; Luke 7:36–50); and the unknown woman caught in adultery (John 7:53–8:11). A homily given by Pope Gregory the Great in the sixth century conflating all these biblical women helped to solidify the misconceptions about Mary Magdalene.[136] Because of these false perceptions of Mary, even the name "Magdalene" has come to be associated with institutions for prostitutes, such as the "Magdalene Laundries" or "Magdalene Asylums" in Ireland in the eighteenth to twentieth centuries. Further besmirching the name is the reality that has come to light in recent times that many of these institutions abused the women who were placed in them. One that attempts to rescue the name is Magdalene House in Chicago, which offers a place of healing for women who are recovering from trafficking, prostitution, addiction, and homelessness.

### *Extracanonical Women Apostles*

In addition to the women in the New Testament who are named and portrayed as apostles, there are many others who were so regarded in the early church. Some of their stories are preserved in extracanonical writings and in legends.

The *Acts of Thecla*, for example, written in Asia Minor in the late second century, tells of how Thecla, a rich aristocratic woman from Iconium, after listening for three days to Paul's preaching, renounced her family, fortune, and fiancé to join him in his apostolic mission. The result is that Paul is banished from the town and Thecla is sentenced to be burned at the stake. She is saved by a storm and sets off with Paul to Antioch of Pisidia. This is only the first of many harrowing adventures for Thecla. Another was her successful fighting off a nobleman who tried to rape her, after which *she* is put on trial for assault, thrown to wild beasts to be eaten, and once again miraculously escapes, when the female beasts protect her. After this, she begins to dress like a man and, with Paul's blessing, continues the itinerant mission until her death near Seleucia.

Devotion to Thecla became widespread throughout Asia Minor and Egypt, particularly among women, who saw her as a model of empowerment. She preached to both men and women (contrary to the injunction against women instructing men in 1 Tim 2:12)[137] and defied the norms of her day by renouncing marriage, baptizing herself, traveling about, and dressing like a man.[138]

Thecla's image has been found painted on walls of tombs, stamped on clay flasks and oil lamps, and engraved on crosses.[139] Like the Samaritan woman, Thecla has been venerated in Orthodox tradition as "apostle and protomartyr among women" and "equal to the apostles in sanctity."[140] Thecla's feast day is celebrated in the Western Rite Orthodox Church on September 23 by those who follow the new calendar; October 6 by those adhering to the old calendar. The Roman Catholic Church no longer lists her in the Calendar of Saints due to doubts about her historicity.[141]

Another woman venerated in the Orthodox Church as "equal of the apostles" is Nino or Nina. The traditions about her are varied. One strand of tradition says she was originally from Cappadocia and that her father, Zabulon, a Roman army chief, relocated the family to Jerusalem, when Nino was twelve years old. Soon after, he left the family for the wilderness of Jordan to take up the life of a monk. Nino's mother was then ordained a deaconess by her brother, Juvenal, the first patriarch of Jerusalem (451–458). She entrusted Nino, her only child, to the care of an elderly woman, Sara Niaphor, who tutored the girl in theology. Subsequently, Juvenal gave her a cross and commissioned her to evangelize wherever she might go. She made her way to Georgia (ancient Iberia), making converts of all who heard her preaching, including Queen Nana and eventually King Mirian, who declared Christianity the official religion.

Nino died in Georgia, having established it as a nation firmly rooted in the faith, earning her the epithet "enlightener of Georgia."[142] The Orthodox Church commemorates her on January 14.

Traditions about women apostles such as Junia, Mary Magdalene, Martha, Photina, Thecla, Nino, and others who brought myriad people to faith through their preaching of the gospel abound. While not all of these may have been historical persons, the traditions attest that there were, indeed, women apostles from the earliest times and, despite the many obstacles they had to overcome, their ministry was effective.

# III

# SEATING ARRANGEMENTS

We see from many New Testament texts that women did have a place at the table in the Jesus movement and in the early church. But where were they seated? Many have the mistaken notion that women never sat at the table; they only prepared and served the meal. Preparing and serving the meal are also of critical importance, as noted above in our comments on Simon's mother-in-law and Jesus's parable of the bakerwoman (Luke 13:20–21 // Matt 13:33). Those roles for women have never been questioned. However, their place at the table has.

## WOMEN HOSTS AND THEIR GUESTS

There is abundant NT evidence that some women were at the head of the table, metaphorically, and perhaps literally, speaking. Women like Mary, the mother of John Mark, in Jerusalem (Acts 12:12), Lydia in Philippi (Acts 16:14, 40), Nympha in Colossae (Col 4:15), Prisca in Corinth and Ephesus (Acts 18; Rom 16:3–5), Martha in Bethany (Luke 10:38–42; John 11:1—12:11), and Phoebe in Cenchreae (Rom 16:1–2), hosted and likely presided over celebrations of the Lord's Supper in the gatherings of believers in their homes.

As hosts, these women would have selected the menu and likely would have pronounced the ritual words of blessing over the bread and cup. Since women were the managers of households, even when the leader of the assembly was male, as Lyn Osiek observed, "to step into a Christian house church was to step into women's world."[1]

I wonder how female hosts of house churches would have heard Jesus's teaching in Luke 14:12–13, "When you give a luncheon or a dinner, do not invite your friends or your brothers or your relatives or rich neighbors, in case they may invite you in return, and you would be repaid. But when you give a banquet, invite the poor, the crippled, the lame, and the blind." In several New Testament texts, women, especially widows, are said to be particularly attentive to the needs of those who were poor. Tabitha, for example, was said to be "devoted to good works and acts of charity" (Acts 9:36).[2] In 1 Timothy 5:10, qualifications for the ministry of widow include being: "well attested for her good works, as one who has brought up children, shown hospitality, washed the saints' feet, helped the afflicted, and devoted herself to doing good in every way." Might it have been that women hosts had less social capital to lose than men and may have found it easy to extend their concern for those who were needy into table companionship with them?

## WOMEN WHO INTRUDE UNINVITED

The reality of women at the table, some in the place of honor, is often overshadowed by stories in the Gospels where women are not at the table, or where their leadership is contested. For example, the story in Luke's Gospel of the woman who comes into the banquet of Simon the Pharisee and pours out her expensive ointment and her tears on Jesus's feet as an extravagant act of love and thanksgiving for having been released from her sins shows a woman who is not a participant in the banquet but an uninvited guest and an object of discussion. She is not at the table but behind Jesus, at his feet, as he is reclining. And in the vignette with Martha and Mary (Luke 10:38–42), the place Mary chooses as a silent learner at Jesus's feet is upheld as "the better part," while Martha's choice of diakonal service is disparaged. The opening verse says that Martha welcomed Jesus into her home,[3] hinting that she is the head of the house and likely the leader of the group of believers that meet there. Martha is worried about the "much *diakonia*," most likely referring to public ministries that men like Luke think should be left to the male disciples. The image that Luke wants us to have is that women belong at the feet, not the head, silently learning, but not taking the lead in interpreting, preaching, and evangelizing. And in Luke's Last Supper scene, only the apostles

(22:14), whom Luke equates with the twelve males named in Luke 9 (vv. 1–6, 10), are at the table.

## AT THE BOSOM OF JESUS

A much different version of the Last Supper scene is found in the Gospel of John. In that Gospel, there is no calling or sending of the Twelve. Instead, disciples, *mathētai*, a diverse group of women and men followers, are mentioned more than seventy times. These are Jesus's "own," whom he loves to the end / completely (*eis telos*, 13:1). Prime among them is the Beloved Disciple,[4] who reclines at the bosom of Jesus, *en tę kolpę tou Iesou* (13:23) at the Last Supper, an expression that recalls the intimacy of the Father and Son described in the prologue (*en tę kolpę tou patros*, 1:18). The image is that of a child nursing at its mother's breast—there is a bit of gender bending here. The intimacy that the Son experiences with the Father, like that of a child at its mother's breast, is the same as that experienced by the Beloved Disciple, that is, every disciple, with Jesus. At the table in John's Gospel are all Jesus's "own," female and male, any of whom can be in the place of honor (in this Gospel, Peter is not at the head).

## TAKING THE LOWEST PLACE[5]

A counter-message is heard, however, in the Gospel of Luke. In 14:7–24, Jesus discourages disciples from taking the place of honor at a banquet, a message that many women have internalized. Jesus criticizes the dining practices whereby guests are seated by rank.[6] At banquets, the host and guests would recline on couches or mats on their left sides, using their right hand to reach the table in the center. The table was u-shaped, a three-sided *triclinium*, meant to provide equal access to the food, conversation, and entertainment.[7] This ideal was not in fact, realized, as each position at the table was assigned and all the guests certainly knew their rank in relation to the others.[8] To be asked by the host to move after taking a place designated for a more honored guest, as depicted in the parable in Luke 14:9, would be a humiliating disgrace. Far better, Jesus advises, is to take the lowest place, and have the host invite you to move up higher. Many women have taken this message to heart and think it is prideful to seek a prominent place at the table. It is critical, however, to keep in mind step number two in Holy Wisdom's cooking class—to be cognizant of one's social location before taking to heart Jesus's admonitions to take the last place and to humble oneself. In Luke 14:7–11, Jesus is addressing the socially well positioned guests of a prominent Pharisee. They can afford to take a humble place; not so for those who are customarily humiliated and excluded.

The teaching in Luke 14:11 concludes, "For all who exalt themselves will be humbled, and those who humble themselves will be exalted." Reversal of status is a theme that resounds throughout the Third Gospel, beginning with Mary's Magnificat at 1:46–55, which praises God for bringing down the mighty from their thrones and lifting up all those who are humiliated and for filling the hungry with good things and sending the rich away empty. However, feminists caution that status reversal does not result in equity; if unequal power structures remain in place, only the characters change. Rather, as Elisabeth Schüssler Fiorenza advanced, to arrive at a community of equal disciples, where all have an equitable place at the table, strategies of empowerment are needed to raise up those at the bottom of domination systems, while those at the top need to relinquish power, privilege, and status.[9]

## SEEN BUT NOT HEARD

Very frequently, Luke portrays Jesus as a participant in a meal, sometimes as guest, other times as host.[10] Luke paints these scenes as typical Greco-Roman style symposia, where there is the dinner and then extended discussion and entertainment.[11]

Women, though present at Greco-Roman banquets, Jewish Passover Seders, and Christian Eucharists, are never portrayed as interlocutors in the Lukan scenes of symposia.[12] While some women who attended banquets would take their leave after the meal and not participate in the symposium that followed, others, especially Roman women of the upper class who were well educated, would have been able interlocutors in the philosophical discussions. There are numerous examples in Greco-

Roman literature where the women who participated in the after-dinner symposia were criticized, even characterized as prostitutes.[13] But we also know of at least one example of a first-century Jewish monastic community in Alexandria, the Therapeutae,[14] described by Philo, in which both male and female members participated in meals together as well as in the after-dinner proceedings.[15] The women and men were segregated, however, by a partition that did not reach the ceiling. This separation allowed for the women to participate in the symposium while also preserving their reputation for chastity.

While women clearly hosted early Christian assemblies and likely pronounced the blessing over the bread and cup,[16] the role of teacher at the symposium following the meal was another matter. At Greco-Roman banquets, the custom was to invite someone other than the host to speak after the meal, usually a noted philosopher or a person trained in rhetorical skills. In Christian assemblies, the invited teacher would have reflected on the Scripture texts that were read, helping those assembled both to understand their meaning and giving spiritual guidance for living them out. Luke's meal scenes show no women participating in the table talk, much less taking on the role of teacher. Luke upholds the ideal of a silent, submissive Greco-Roman matron, such as Mary who listens docilely at the feet of Jesus (10:38–42), and discourages women from taking up the ministries of teaching and preaching.[17]

Feminists recognize that Luke is telling only part of the story and he is telling it slant. We try to unearth the rest of the story and look to its potential for nourishing a church wherein all have a place at the table, where women are just as able as men to be at the head and are recognized as authoritative interpreters of the Scriptures and wise spiritual guides.

# IV

# RESHAPING THE TABLE

As we are picturing the table, I suggest that some of our Christian art has done us a disservice both in giving us false depictions and in stymying our imagination. Leonardo DaVinci's ***Last Supper***, for example, has both the shape of the table and the guest list all wrong. Jesus and the Twelve would not all have been on one side of a long table (as if to say "All you guys who want to be in the picture, get on this side of the table"). As mentioned above, dinner tables for more formal events in Jesus's day would be three-sided ***triclinia***. We might ponder: how would Holy Wisdom shape her table? Would it be long and square, with a clear head and foot and ranked seating? I think not!

## CHURCH IN THE ROUND

What if the table instead were round, where there was no head or foot, where all had an equal place, even though with distinct roles? Decades ago, Letty Russell elaborated on what a "church in the round" might look like and how it might function: a circular table around which the most disadvantaged people of the world are gathered in response to an open and inclusive hospitality.[1] The Fourth Gospel comes closest to giving us an idea of how this could be. In that Gospel, there is no group of twelve men who become the lead apostles; all are beloved disciples, friends of Jesus, a relationship that implies equality in status. In John's Gospel, Peter is not given keys to the kingdom (as in Matt 16:19) and it is Martha who makes the declaration of Jesus as Messiah, not Peter (John 11:27; cf. Mark 8:29; Matt 16:16; Luke 9:20). In the community of the Beloved Disciple, women play other key roles: Jesus's mother helps birth Jesus's public ministry at Cana and is among the women at the foot of the cross, who act as midwives, if you will, in rebirthing the community to carry on Jesus's mission; the Samaritan woman is the model apostle, bringing her townspeople to belief in Jesus; Mary of Bethany prefigures Jesus's washing of the feet of his disciples by anointing his feet; Mary Magdalene, in coming alone to the tomb, represents the whole community of believers, as she is the first to encounter the Risen Christ and to be commissioned to proclaim the good news. As Sandra Schneiders has observed, all these examples point toward the reality that there were women evangelists, prophets, teachers, apostles, ministers, hosts, leaders in that community of believers—you don't tell the story that way unless there are actual women in the community who are performing these roles.

In calling for a table of a different shape, we recognize that deep structural change is needed; it will not do just to invite women to the current tables; the structures of church and of ministry themselves need radical reshaping by Wisdom's friends.

## A SYNODAL CHURCH

One hopeful step forward toward reshaping the table may be found in the current invitation by Pope Francis to participate in synodal processes to cocreate the church of the future. The word *synod* combines the Greek preposition *syn*, "with" and the noun *hodos*, "way, path," yielding the meaning "together on the way." Synodality concerns a manner of being together on the way that is calling us to a deep level of conversion from a church that has evolved into pyramidal structures and top-down decision-making into a church that listens to and walks side by side with one another, with hearts wide open, allowing ourselves to be changed by the other in the encounter and, ultimately, to become a church that is focused on mercy.

An attitude of synodality means seeking out and listening to the voices on the peripheries who have diverse experiences of God's mercy. Recently, Cardinal Joseph Tobin of Newark, New Jersey, offered this image of how Pope John XXIII started moving the church toward synodal processes with Vatican II. Pope John used the metaphor of opening the windows to let in the fresh air. But more than that, Cardinal Tobin suggests that opening the windows also lets in the voices from the streets.[2]

In the last two synods that Pope Francis has called, the Synod on Young People in 2018 and the Synod on the Amazon in 2019, he has done this very thing: he has drawn into the center the voices of those not usually heard: the young and indigenous persons in a remote part of the world. And in October 2023 there will be a synod on the theme: "For a synodal Church: communion, participation, and mission"—a synod on synodality!

This direction in which Pope Francis is leading us is hardly new; we can see clear intimations of synodal processes and ways of thinking in the NT.[3] In the Gospels, as Jesus moves throughout towns and villages healing and proclaiming the good news, his disciples, both women and men, are together with him on the way and learning from him how to sustain their oneness as the Jesus movement grows. The Acts of the Apostles shows us at least three ways in which the women and men who were committed to walking together as they had with Jesus tried to deepen their synodality: they prayed together, broke bread together, and held all their possessions in common (Acts 2:44–47; 4:32–37).

These practices prepared them for making very difficult decisions, such as when the Jesus movement, composed predominantly of faithful Jews, began to attract more and more Gentiles. As Acts 15 tells it, when divisions emerged over whether Gentile believers must be circumcised and observe the dietary regulations of the Torah, Paul and Barnabas were sent by the church of Antioch to go up to Jerusalem to discuss the matter with the leaders there. In the debate that ensued, the leaders solicited testimony from diverse perspectives. As they discerned the way forward, they turned to the Scriptures for guidance and invoked the Holy Spirit. A compromise solution was reached, and a letter was read to all the brothers and sisters in Antioch, who received it with joy. This decision-making process has some intimations of synodality, but today feminists ask: Were any of the women's voices listened to? Were young people consulted? Those on the peripheries?

The intimations of synodality in the early church and our movement in that direction today are also confirmed by what we are learning from new science. As we move from a Newtonian mechanistic and materialistic view of the universe in which it was thought that studying the parts leads to understanding the whole, we are shifting into the mindset of new science that focuses on wholism rather than parts and gives attention to relationship and the connectedness of all creation.[4] Leaders using such synodal approaches focus on eliciting possibility, generosity, and the gifts of the whole group, valuing diversity and risking experimentation rather than problem solving, fear, and retribution in a command and control model.[5] Building circles of friends and fostering networks of compassion is another approach to leadership that generates new ideas and new ways of responding to the mission.[6]

In his letter to the Philippians, St. Paul eloquently expresses one more absolutely essential element for embodying synodality in our relationships with one another. He urges them and us to look not only to our own interests, but to the interests of others (Phil 2:4). He invites us to pattern our lives on the self-emptying that is modeled on Christ's life, who moved from life with God, to life with humanity, and then through death to new life (Phil 2:6–11).

In the more than five decades since Vatican Council II urged us on a path toward renewal, women religious such as Sisters Madeleva have been in the forefront of reshaping models of leadership. Many of our congregations have experimented with circular models of governance and shared leadership. We have learned much about what works and what pitfalls to try to avoid. Both women religious and lay women leaders who are shifting patterns in the workplace have much wisdom to offer the wider church about synodal models.

If the new synodal process begun in our day succeeds, this is a very good first step toward reshaping the table of Holy Wisdom where all are invited to the banquet, all contribute to the meal, and all have equal access to her sumptuous fare.

# V

# CONCLUSION

As we find ourselves in a world hungry for peace, justice, mercy, and flourishing of all creation, one essential way to satisfy these longings is to engage a feminist liberationist approach to biblical interpretation. Learning such skills from Holy Wisdom and her friends not only gives us new ways of thinking and praying but leads to transformative action that has the potential to change unjust relationship patterns and structures.

In this short volume, it seems like we've only gotten through the appetizers. If you're hungry for more, there are many good resources that serve up hearty, satisfying feminist fare to which I hope you'll turn. The works cited in this volume can help you become a master feminist chef, not only providing you with some tried and true recipes but also giving you the ingredients to experiment with new feminist fare. As well, having learned from Holy Wisdom, we become emboldened to reject interpretations that are misogynistic or kyriarchal as unpalatable and no longer tolerable. For our starving world, only nourishing fare that intends the flourishing of all life on the planet will do. Almost eight decades ago, Sister Madeleva "forever changed the face of Catholic theology."[1] If one woman listening to the promptings of Holy Wisdom could do that, imagine what all of us together can do!

# NOTES

## I

1. Barbara E. Reid and Shelly Matthews, *Luke 1–9*, WCS 43A (Collegeville, MN: Liturgical Press, 2021), xxiii.

2. Alice Walker coined the term (*In Search of Our Mothers' Gardens: Womanist Prose* [New York: Harcourt Brace Jovanovich, 1967, 1983]). See also Katie G. Cannon, "The Emergence of Black Feminist Consciousness," in *Feminist Interpretation of the Bible*, ed. Letty M. Russell (Philadelphia: Westminster, 1985), 30–40; Renita Weems, *Just a Sister Away: A Womanist Vision of Women's Relationships in the Bible* (San Diego: Lura Media, 1988); Nyasha Junior, *An Introduction to Womanist Biblical Interpretation* (Louisville: Westminster John Knox, 2015).

3. Ada María Isasi-Díaz (*Mujerista Theology: A Theology for the Twenty-First Century* [Maryknoll, NY: Orbis Books, 1996]) is credited with coining the term *mujerista*. Others, such as María Pilar Aquino, Daisy L. Machado, and Jeanette Rodríguez, eds., *A Reader in Latina Feminist Theology* (Austin: University of Texas Press, 2002), have used "Latina feminist." On Latinx approaches to biblical interpretation, see Francisco Lozada, Jr., "Latinx Biblical Interpretation," *Jerome*

*Biblical Commentary for the 21st Century* (London: Bloomsbury T & T Clark, 2022), 2111–18.

4. In what follows, I rely on the seven steps outlined by Elisabeth Schüssler Fiorenza in *Wisdom Ways: Introducing Feminist Biblical Interpretation* (Maryknoll, NY: Orbis Books, 2001); see also Barbara E. Reid, *Wisdom's Feast: An Invitation to Feminist Interpretation of the Scriptures* (Grand Rapids, MI: Eerdmans, 2016), 8–12.

5. This approach was first advocated by Latin American liberation theologians, such as Gustavo Gutiérrez, *A Theology of Liberation* (Maryknoll, NY: Orbis Books, 1988).

6. *Kyriarchy* means "rule of the masters or lords" (derived from the Greek words *kyrios*, "lord," and *archein*, "to rule"). It was first introduced by Elisabeth Schüssler Fiorenza as a better term than *patriarchy*, "rule of the fathers," to speak of interlocking systems of domination and power relations. Not all men are at the top of the pyramid of power as masters. See further Schüssler Fiorenza, *Wisdom Ways*, 102–34.

7. Phyllis Trible, *Texts of Terror: Literary-Feminist Readings of Biblical Narratives* (Philadelphia: Fortress, 1984).

8. See her diagram in Schüssler Fiorenza, *Wisdom Ways*, 194.

9. See further, "One Thousand Years of Feminist Bible Criticism," in Gerda Lerner, *The Creation of Feminist Consciousness: From the Middle Ages to Eighteen-Seventy* (New York: Oxford University Press, 1993), 138–66; Susanne Scholz, "From the 'Woman's Bible' to the 'Women's Bible,' The History of Feminist Approaches to the Hebrew Bible," in *Introducing the Women's Hebrew Bible*, IFT 13 (New York: T&T Clark, 2007), 12–32; Marion Ann Taylor and Agnes Choi, eds., *Handbook of Women Biblical Interpreters: A Historical and Biographical Guide* (Grand Rapids, MI: Baker Academic, 2012).

10. This sketch is an adaptation of my Editor's Introduction that appears in each volume of the Wisdom Commentary series.

11. Madrid, Escorial MS, a II 9, f. 90 v., as cited in Lerner, *Feminist Consciousness*, 140.

12. See Judith R. Baskin, "Women and Post-Biblical Commentary," in *The Torah: A Women's Commentary*, ed. Tamara Cohn Eskenazi and Andrea L. Weiss (New York: URJ Press and Women of Reform Judaism, The Federation of Temple Sisterhoods, 2008), xlix–lv, at lii.

13. See Hildegard of Bingen, *De Operatione Dei*, 1.4.100; PL 197:885bc, as cited in Lerner, *Feminist Consciousness*, 142–43. See also Barbara Newman, *Sister of Wisdom: St. Hildegard's Theology of the Feminine* (Berkeley: University of California Press, 1987).

14. Emily Taitz, Sondra Henry, and Cheryl Tallan, eds., *JPS Guide to Jewish Women 600 B.C.E.–1900 C.E.* (Philadelphia: JPS, 2003), 110–11.

15. See further Taylor and Choi, *Handbook of Women Biblical Interpreters*, 127–32.

16. Margaret Fell (1614–1702) was one of the founders of the Religious Society of Friends (Quakers). Her major work, *Women's Speaking Justified, Proved and Allowed by the Scriptures*, published in London in 1667, gave a systematic feminist reading of all biblical texts pertaining to women.

17. See further Sarah Grimké, *Letters on the Equality of the Sexes and the Condition of Woman* (Boston: Isaac Knapp, 1838).

18. A rendition of her speech can be viewed at http://www.fordham.edu/halsall/mod/sojtruth-woman.asp.

19. The full title is *The Women of Israel or Characters and Sketches from the Holy Scriptures and Jewish History Illustrative*

*of the Past History, Present Duty, and Future Destiny of the Hebrew Females, as Based on the Word of God.*

20. See further Eskenazi and Weiss, *The Torah: A Women's Commentary*, xxxviii; Taylor and Choi, *Handbook of Women Biblical Interpreters*, 31–37.

21. Elisabeth Schüssler Fiorenza with Shelly Matthews, eds., *Searching the Scriptures*, vol. 1: *A Feminist Introduction* (New York: Crossroad, 1993); vol. 2: *A Feminist Commentary* (New York: Crossroad, 1994).

22. German edition: *Kompendium Feministische Bibelauslegung*, ed. Luise Schottroff and Marie-Theres Wacker (Gütersloh: Gütersloher Verlagshaus, 2007); English: *Feminist Biblical Interpretation. A Compendium of Critical Commentary on the Books of the Bible and Related Literature*, transl. Lisa E. Dahill, Everett R. Kalin, Nancy Lukens, Linda M. Maloney, Barbara Rumscheidt, Martin Rumscheidt, and Tina Steiner (Grand Rapids, MI: Eerdmans, 2012).

23. The English volumes are published by the Society of Biblical Literature (Atlanta): *Torah*, ed. Irmtraud Fischer and Mercedes Navarro Puerto (2011); *Feminist Biblical Studies in the Twentieth Century*, ed. Elisabeth Schüssler Fiorenza (2014); *The Writings and Later Wisdom Books*, ed. Christl M. Maier and Nuria Calduch-Benages (2014); *Gospels: Narrative and History*, ed. Mercedes Navarro Puerto and Marinella Perroni; Amy-Jill Levine (English ed.); *The High Middle Ages*, ed. Kari Elisabeth Børresen and Adriana Valerio (2015); *Early Jewish Writings*, ed. Eileen Schuller and Marie-Theres Wacker (2017); *Faith and Feminism in Nineteenth-Century Religious Communities,* ed. Michaela Sohn-Kronthaler and Ruth Albrecht (2019); *Faith and Feminism in Nineteenth-Century Religious Communities,* ed. Michaela Sohn-Kronthaler and Ruth Albrecht (2020); *Prophecy and Gender in the Hebrew Bible*, ed. L. Juliana Claasens and Irmtraud Fischer (2021);

and *Rabbinic Literature,* ed. Tal Ilan Lorena Miralles-Maciá and Ronit Nikolsky (2022). For further information, see http://www.bibleandwomen.org.

## II

1. A few examples of the use of the metaphor by contemporary feminists: Deborah M. Kolb, Carol Frohlinger, Judith Williams, *Her Place at the Table: A Woman's Guide to Negotiating Five Key Challenges to Leadership Success* (San Francisco: Jossey-Bass, 2004); Tina Beattie, "A Place at the Table: The Story of *Catholic Women Speak*," *Commonweal* 143, no. 7 (April 15, 2016), https://www.commonwealmagazine.org/place-table; "A Place at the Table: Syrian Women's Group Advising UN Special Envoy During Peace Talks," https://www.msn.com/en-sg/entertainment/story/a-place-at-the-table-syrian-womens-group-advising-un-special-envoy-during-peace-talks/vi-BBqV4Wt.

2. See Mark 3:13–19; 6:6b–13 // Matt 10:1–15 // Luke 6:12–16; 9:1–6 on the call and sending forth of the Twelve.

3. BDAG, 609.

4. The noun ***mathētēs*** occurs approximately 73 times in Matthew; 47 times in Mark; 38 times in Luke; 78 times in John; 28 times in the Acts of the Apostles. It does not occur in the Pauline letters. The verb form, ***mathēteuō***, "to teach," occurs only in Matthew (13:52; 27:57; 28:19) and once in Acts 14:21.

5. Peter at Mark 8:27–29 // Matt 16:13–15 // Luke 9:18–20; Mark 14:33; 16:7; Matt 17:6, 10, 13; 19:27; 26:20, 36, 40, 45; Luke 22:31; John 6:68; 13:8–11, 24, 36–38; 18:10, 15; 20:2; 21:2. At times his name is given as Simon, as at Luke 22:31; sometimes as Simon Peter, as at John 18:10, 15; 20:2; 21:2. Judas at Matt 26:20; John 12:4; 13:26–30.

James and John at Mark 14:33; Matt 17:6, 10, 13; 26:36, 45; Luke 9:54; John 21:2. Sometimes James and John are denoted as the sons of Zebedee without giving their names: Matt 26:36; John 21:2. Joseph of Arimathea at Matt 27:57; John 19:38. Andrew at John 6:8 (at John 1:37–40, Andrew is one of John's disciples who follows Jesus). Philip and Thomas at John 20:24–26; 21:2. Nathanael at John 21:2.

6. D. A. Carson, e.g., asserts, "The appearance to Mary Magdalene is not counted, since that was not an appearance *to his disciples*." D. A. Carson, *The Gospel According to John* (Grand Rapids, MI: Eerdmans, 1991), 675; italics original. Similarly, Rudolf K. Bultmann, *The Gospel of John. A Commentary*, trans. G. R. Beasley-Murray, R. W. N. Hoare, and J. K. Riches (Philadelphia: Westminster, 1971), 706; so also C. K. Barrett, *The Gospel according to St. John: An Introduction with Commentary and Notes on the Greek Text* (London: S.P.C.K., 1955), 582; and Claudia Setzer, *Jewish Responses to Early Christians: History and Polemics, 30–150 C.E.* (Philadelphia: Fortress, 1994), 268.

7. Adele Reinhartz, "Women in the Johannine Community: An Exercise in Historical Imagination," in *A Feminist Companion to John*, vol. 2, FCNTECW 5, ed. Amy-Jill Levine with Marianne Blickenstaff (Sheffield: Sheffield Academic, 2003), 14–33, here 28–29 n. 24. Reinhartz sees two ways in which *mathētai* is used in the Fourth Gospel: (1) broadly as referring to followers of and believers in Jesus as the Christ and Son of God; and (2) followers who accompanied Jesus on his travels and were his more regular audience (27).

8. John P. Meier, *A Marginal Jew: Rethinking the Historical Jesus, Vol. III: Companions and Competitors*, ABRL (New York: Doubleday, 2001), 72. Meier sees Jesus as an eschatological prophet and miracle worker in the likeness of Elijah

and looks to the story of Elijah's call of Elisha (1 Kgs 19:19–21), for the pattern for Jesus's calling of his disciples.

9. Meier, *A Marginal Jew*, vol. III, 76–77.

10. Meier, *A Marginal Jew*, vol. III, 77.

11. Meier, *A Marginal Jew*, vol. III, 79.

12. The section that follows is an expansion of my essay, "The Happy Few Plus a Few More," in *The Figure of Jesus in History and Theology: Essays in Honor of John Meier*, CBQ Imprints 1, ed. Vincent T. M. Skemp and Kelley Coblentz Bautch (Washington, DC: The Catholic Biblical Association, 2020), 114–26.

13. Elaine M. Wainwright, *Towards a Feminist Critical Reading of the Gospel According to Matthew*, BZNW 60 (Berlin: deGruyter, 1991), 177–91.

14. See Victoria Phillips, "Full Disclosure: Towards a Complete Characterization of the Women Who Followed Jesus in the Gospel According to Mark," in *Transformative Encounters: Jesus and Women Re-viewed*, ed. Ingrid Rosa Kitzberger, BibInt 43 (Leiden: Brill, 2000), 13–32, and more recently Warren Carter, *Mark*, WCS 42 (Collegeville, MN: Liturgical Press, 2019), lxiv–lxvii, who argue that the crucifixion scene creates a retrospective effect for readers engaging the whole Gospel, so that whenever disciples are mentioned in the Gospel, we should envision women among them.

15. Some scholars, such as John Meier (*Marginal Jew*, vol. 3, 76) see in this vignette a "potentially shocking picture of women" traveling around in the company of men unchaperoned. For Meier, this image goes against the grain of Luke's aim to present Christianity as a respectable movement. However, Luke does not justify the women traveling and seems unconcerned about the supposed scandal it would cause. Likewise, he makes no explanation for Mary traveling alone from Nazareth to visit Elizabeth in Judea (1:39), a journey

that would have taken approximately four days on foot. Fourteenth-century writer Ludolph of Saxony, in his widely read book, *Vita Domini nostri Jesu Christi ex quatuor evangeliis*, resolved the problem by saying that a train of virgins and angels accompanied Mary to protect her. Bruce J. Malina and Richard L. Rohrbaugh (*Social Science Commentary on the Synoptic Gospels* [Minneapolis: Fortress, 1992]) suggest that Mary "considers the son she conceives as apotropaic, clearly capable of warding off evil" (291). Another way to interpret Luke 8:1–3 is to view the women as homebound supporters rather than unchaperoned itinerants. See "Women, Itinerancy and the Criteria of Authenticity in John Meier's *Marginal Jew*," in *The Figure of Jesus in History and Theology*, 90–113. Alternatively, Luke may be describing "day trips from home bases," as advanced by Jane D. Schaberg and Sharon H. Ringe, "Gospel of Luke," in *Women's Bible Commentary*, ed. Carol A. Newsom, Sharon H. Ringe, and Jacqueline E. Lapsley, 3rd ed. (Louisville: Westminster John Knox, 2012), 506.

16. Similarly, Luke 22:27, "I am among you as one who serves [*ho diakonōn*]."

17. The disciples are named as the audience in 18:1. In the Markan parallel, Jesus addresses this saying (9:37) to the twelve (9:35). In Luke, the disciples (9:43) are the audience for the saying (9:48).

18. The disciples are named as the audience in 24:1.

19. Zacchaeus would also qualify, as he "was happy to welcome him [Jesus]" (Luke 19:6) to his home.

20. See also the parable of the builder, which concludes, "Everyone then who hears these words of mine and acts on them will be like a wise man who built his house on rock" (Matt 7:24; cf. Luke 6:49).

21. The Greek verb *miseō*, "hate," does not mean to actively despise, but rather "be disinclined to, disfavor, dis-

regard, in contrast to preferential treatment" (BDAG, 653). Matthew captures this meaning in his version of the saying: "Whoever loves father or mother more than me is not worthy of me; and whoever loves son or daughter more than me is not worthy of me" (10:37).

22. In Luke's Gospel, there is no mention of men related to Mary and Martha; only that the two women are sisters (10:38–42). It is only in John's Gospel we learn that they have a brother, Lazarus (11:1—12:8). Still, no indication is given of the sisters' marital status.

23. See, e.g., Sheila E. McGinn, "The Acts of Thecla," in *Searching the Scriptures*, vol. 2: *A Feminist Commentary*, ed. Elisabeth Schüssler Fiorenza with the assistance of Ann Brock and Shelly Matthews (New York: Crossroad, 1994), 800–828; Virginia Burrus, *Chastity as Autonomy: Women in the Stories of the Apocryphal Acts* (Lewiston, NY: Mellen, 1987); Bonnie Bowman Thurston, *The Widows: A Women's Ministry in the Early Church* (Minneapolis: Fortress, 1989).

24. See further "The Cross That Should Not Be Taken Up," in Reid and Matthews, *Luke 1–9*, 285–86, and Barbara E. Reid, *Taking Up the Cross. New Testament Interpretations Through Latina and Feminist Eyes* (Minneapolis: Fortress, 2007); Spanish translation: *Reconsiderar la cruz. Interpretación latinoamericana y feminista del Nuevo Testamento* (Estella [Navarra]: Editorial Verbo Divino, 2009).

25. Joseph A. Fitzmyer, *The Gospel According to Luke I–IX*, AB 28 (Garden City, NY: Doubleday, 1981), 429–30.

26. See below, p. 119n123 for those who think Mark and Matthew intend one of the Marys at the crucifixion to be Jesus's mother.

27. In his second Letter to the Corinthians, Paul himself lists the "afflictions, hardships, calamities" he has endured:

"beatings, imprisonments, riots, labors, sleepless nights, hunger" (2 Cor 6:4–5).

28. Christian communities of women and men religious today still try to live in this manner. In Israel, collective communities, kibbutzim (plural of kibbutz; the Hebrew word קיבוץ means "gathering, clustering"), have a similar aim.

29. For a more detailed analysis of the characteristics of discipleship and the depiction of women in Luke and Acts, see Barbara E. Reid, *Choosing the Better Part? Women in the Gospel of Luke* (Collegeville, MN: Liturgical Press, 1996), esp. 21–54.

30. In Paul's letters, she is called Prisca; Luke names her Priscilla, a diminutive form. Linda M. Maloney (*Acts*, WCS 45 [Collegeville, MN: Liturgical Press, 2022], 255 n. 1) remarks that Luke "has a penchant for using diminutive forms of names: Priscilla for Prisca, Silas for Silvanus. Here it may represent a (vain!) attempt to reduce Prisca to secondary status since she is almost an afterthought at her first appearance in v. 2, but by v. 18 she is in first place, and there she remains (cp. 18:26)."

31. Maloney, *Acts*, 262.

32. Maloney, *Acts*, 262.

33. For more detail, see chap. 5, "The Missionary Artisan Priscilla and the Universal Praise That Is Her Due (18:1–3, 18–19, 24–28), in Ivoni Richter Reimer, *Women in the Acts of the Apostles. A Feminist Liberationist Perspective* (trans. Linda M. Maloney; Minneapolis: Fortress, 1995), 195–226.

34. This happens in four of the six instances in which they are named: Acts 18:18, 26; Rom 16:3; 2 Tim 4:19. In Acts 18:2 and 1 Cor 16:19 Aquila is named first.

35. Others whom Paul names as coworkers are Urbanus (Rom 16:9), Timothy (Rom 16:21; 1 Thess 3:2), Apollos (1 Cor 3:9); Titus (2 Cor 8:23), Epaphroditus (Phil 2:25), Euo-

dia, Syntyche and Clement (Phil 4:2–3), Philemon (Phlm 1), Mark, Aristarchus, Demas, and Luke (Phlm 24).

36. It is important to recognize that each evangelist crafts his own portrait of the disciples, and each has his own take on women's participation in the Jesus movement. On women in the Gospel of Mark, see Mercedes Navarro Puerto, "Female Disciples in Mark? The 'Problematizing' of a Concept," in *Gospels: Narrative and History, The Bible and Women: An Encyclopedia of Exegesis and Cultural History* 2.1, ed. Mercedes Navarro Puerto and Marinella Perroni. English edition, ed. Amy-Jill Levine (Atlanta: SBL Press, 2015), 145–72, who provides a list of the most important studies on women disciples in Mark. See also comments by Warren Carter, *Mark*, lxiv–lxvii. For women in Matthew, see Amy-Jill Levine, "The Gospel of Matthew: Between Breaking and Continuity," in *Gospels: Narrative and History*, 121–44; Elaine M. Wainwright, *Towards a Feminist Critical Reading of the Gospel According to Matthew*; In-Cheol Shin, "Matthew's Designation of the Role of Women as Indirectly Adherent Disciples," *Neot* 41 (2007): 399–415; Baby Parambi, *The Discipleship of the Women in the Gospel according to Matthew: An Exegetical Theological Study of Matt 27:51b–56, 57–61 and 28:1–10*, Tesi Gregoriana, Serie Teologia 94 (Rome: Pontificia Università Gregoriana, 2003). For the Gospel of Luke, see "Luke: Friend of Women or Most Dangerous Book in the Bible?," in Reid and Matthews, *Luke 1–9*, lxii–lxvii, and other sources cited therein. For the Gospel of John, see Colleen M. Conway, *Men and Women in the Fourth Gospel: Gender and Johannine Characterization*, SBLDS 167 (Atlanta: SBL, 1999); Margaret M. Beirne, *Women and Men in the Fourth Gospel: A Genuine Discipleship of Equals*, JSNTSup 242 (London: Sheffield Academic, 2003); Adele Reinhartz, "Women in the Johannine Community: An Exercise in Historical Imagination," in *A Feminist Companion to John*, vol. 2,

14–33; Mary Coloe, *John 1–10* and *John 11–21*, WCS 44A and 44B (Collegeville, MN: Liturgical Press, 2021).

37. The first known instance of ***diakonein*** dates to the fifth century, where the historian Herodotus and other classical Greek writers use it to refer to waiting at table (*Herod.* 4.154.3; Aristoph. *Ach.* 1015–16; Diod. *S.*, 5.28.4).

38. See Plat. *Leg.* 7.805e; Plut. *Adulat.* 22.2.63d.

39. John N. Collins, *DIAKONIA: Re-interpreting the Ancient Sources* (New York: Oxford University Press, 1990).

40. Similarly, Matthew 23:11: "The greatest among you will be your servant [***diakonos***]."

41. Portions of this section are adapted from Barbara E. Reid and Shelly Matthews, *Luke 1–9*, WCS 43A (Collegeville, MN: Liturgical Press, 2021), 153–58.

42. In 1 Cor 9:5, Paul speaks of Cephas (Aramaic for Peter) and other apostles being "accompanied by a believing wife [***adelphēn gynaika***, lit. a "sister wife"]," which would indicate that Peter's wife was alive at the time Paul was writing. An alternative interpretation is offered by some early church fathers who understood the expression ***adelphēn gynaika*** to refer to a woman minister, not necessarily a wife (see Jerome, *Ad. Jovinian* 1.26; Clement of Alexandria, *Stromata* 3.6). Clement preserves a tradition that Peter's wife was martyred in Rome (*Stromata* 7.11).

43. A few of many instances where ***anistēmi*** is used of Jesus's resurrection are Luke 24:46; Acts 2:24; ***egeirō*** in Acts 5:30; 10:40; 1 Cor 6:14, and many others.

44. See, e.g., Mary Ann Tolbert, "Mark," in *The Women's Bible Commentary*, ed. Carol A. Newsom and Sharon H. Ringe (Louisville: Westminster John Knox, 1992), 267; Luise Schottroff, *Let the Oppressed Go Free: Feminist Perspectives on the New Testament* (Louisville: Westminster John Knox, 1993), 80–118; Marla Selvidge, "And Those Who Followed

Feared' (Mark 10:32)," *CBQ* 45 (1983): 396–400; Elisabeth Meier Tetlow, *Women and Ministry in the New Testament: Called to Serve* (Lanham, MD: University Press of America, 1985), 97; Schüssler Fiorenza, *In Memory of Her: A Feminist Theological Reconstruction of Christian Origins* (New York: Crossroad, 1983), 320–21.

45. Elaine M. Wainwright, *Women Healing/Healing Women: The Genderization of Healing in Early Christianity*, Bible World (London: Equinox, 2006), 111.

46. In Mark 1:29, Simon, Andrew, James, and John tell Jesus about her; in Luke 4:38, an unnamed "they" ask him.

47. Elaine M. Wainwright, *Towards a Feminist Critical Reading of the Gospel According to Matthew*, 177–91. See also Wainwright, *Women Healing/Healing Women*, 143–46.

48. See further the analysis by Deborah Krause, "Simon Peter's Mother-in-Law—Disciple or Domestic Servant? Feminist Biblical Hermeneutics and the Interpretation of Mark 1.29–31," in *A Feminist Companion to Mark*, ed. Amy-Jill Levine with Marianne Blickenstaff, FCNTECW 2 (Sheffield: Sheffield Academic, 2001), 37–53. Krause concludes: "Mark's Gospel preserves traditions that reveal women in traditionally bound roles of domestic servitude, while at the same time preserving traditions that reveal women in liberated roles of equal discipleship" (50). See also Winsome Munro, who had previously made a similar argument in "Women Disciples in Mark?," *CBQ* 44 (1982): 225–41. See also Matthews and Reid, *Luke 1–9*, 157–58.

49. See Amy-Jill Levine, *Short Stories by Jesus: The Enigmatic Stories of a Controversial Rabbi* (San Francisco: HarperOne, 2014), who sees a connection between Luke 13:20–21 and the prediction of Sarah's pregnancy by the visitors in Genesis 18: "the idea of hiding yeast and of the dough rising

on its own can suggest insemination and then pregnancy" (24).

50. The phrase *basileia tou theou*, usually translated "kingdom of God," presents a number of difficulties from a feminist perspective. First, *kingdom* can imply a place with fixed geographical boundaries, whereas the expression in the Gospels means "kingly rule" or "reign," more a way of being in which divine power works in the world through people who act as Torah and Jesus instruct. Another difficulty with the translation "kingdom of God" is that it implies that God is male, and God's power is expressed in a monarchical top-down pattern. In Jesus's preaching and teaching, he offered instead, images of God that were inclusive and expressions of divine power that were both authoritative and empowering toward the flourishing of all creation. To try to capture better this sense of *basileia*, some feminists have experimented with expressions such as "kin-dom," "rule," "reign," "realm," "empire," "domain," and "commonweal." Others prefer simply to leave it untranslated: *basileia*. See further Elisabeth Schüssler Fiorenza, "The Basileia Vision of Jesus as the Praxis of Inclusive Wholeness," in *In Memory of Her*, 118–30.

51. The word *ekrypsen* in 13:21 literally means "hid," as rendered by KJV and RSV, for example. Many translations, such as the NRSV, NABRE, and NIV, obscure the reference to divine action, rendering *ekrypsen* as "mixed" or "mixed in."

52. See below on Women Hosts and Their Guests.

53. See Luise Schottroff, *Lydia's Impatient Sisters: A Feminist Social History of Early Christianity* (Louisville: Westminster John Knox, 1995), 85.

54. There is also a scene unique to Luke, where a great number of the people follow Jesus on the way to the cross, "and among them were women who were beating their breasts and wailing for him" (23:27).

55. There is no punctuation in the Greek, so the number of women is not clear. Sandra M. Schneiders, e.g., sees three, reading Jesus's mother's sister as being Mary the wife of Clopas. She makes a convincing argument that there is no fourth person (usually thought to be male) who joins the scene in 19:26; the disciple whom Jesus loved is among the three already listed. Mary Magdalene or Mary Magdalene together with Mary of Clopas embody the community of the Beloved Disciple (*Written That You May Believe. Encountering Jesus in the Fourth Gospel*, rev. and expanded ed. [New York: Crossroad, 2003], 238–43).

56. For an analysis of the significance of the healing from demon possession, see Reid and Matthews, "The Women and Their Demons," in *Luke 1–9*, 252–55.

57. E.g., Ben Witherington III, "On the Road with Mary Magdalene, Joanna, Susanna, and Other Disciples—Luke 8:1–3," *ZNW* 70 (1979): 243–48. The setting in Luke 8:1–3 is not the home, as in the episode with Simon's mother-in-law, where *diēkonoun* more likely refers to domestic serving. Here, the women are in open space as traveling missionaries.

58. Luke 11:21; 12:15, 33, 44; 14:33; 16:1; 19:8; Acts 4:32.

59. These women financiers were not unique. The Pharisees were known to have received considerable financial support from women; see Tal Ilan, "The Attraction of Aristocratic Jewish Women to Pharisaism during the Second Temple Period," *HTR* 88 (1995): 1–33. See below on Phoebe, who was a benefactor of Paul (Rom 16:2). See also Carolyn Osiek, "Women Patrons in the Life of House Churches," in Carolyn Osiek and Margaret Y. MacDonald, with Janet H. Tulloch, *A Woman's Place: House Churches in Earliest Christianity* (Minneapolis: Fortress, 2006), 194–219.

60. Women could inherit money and property (Num 27:8), and they earned money as weavers, midwives, doctors, hairdressers, wet nurses, masseuses, attendants, and musicians, for example. See further Jan Gardner, *Women in Roman Law and Society* (Bloomington & Indianapolis: Indiana University Press, 1986), 233–55. In Acts 16, Lydia works with purple (luxury) goods; in Acts 18:3 Prisca is a leather worker along with her husband, Aquila. See further Moshe Meiselman, *Jewish Woman in Jewish Law* (New York: KTAV, 1978), 84–95.

61. Scholars debate whether Lydia herself was well off, as asserted by Shelly Matthews, *First Converts: Rich Pagan Women and the Rhetoric of Mission in Early Judaism and Christianity. Contraversions, Jews and Other Differences* (Stanford: Stanford University Press, 2001), 85–89, or whether she was a poor woman who produced luxury goods for others, as argued by Luise Schottroff, "Lydia: A New Quality of Power," in *Let the Oppressed Go Free: Feminist Perspectives on the New Testament*, trans. Annemarie S. Kidder (Louisville: Westminster/John Knox, 1993), 131–37, and Ivoni Richter Reimer, *Women in the Acts of the Apostles: A Feminist Liberation Perspective*, trans. Linda M. Maloney (Minneapolis: Fortress, 1995), 98–130. Given Luke's predilection for rich women patrons (e.g., Luke 8:3; Acts 12:12; 17:4, 12), it is more likely that Lydia is meant to be seen as one of them.

62. See Katharine Bain, *Women's Socioeconomic Status and Religious Leadership in Asia Minor in the First Two Centuries C.E.* (Minneapolis: Fortress, 2014).

63. This interpretation was first proposed by Elisabeth Schüssler Fiorenza, "A Feminist Critical Interpretation for Liberation: Martha and Mary: Luke 10:38–42," *Religion and Intellectual Life* 3 (1986): 21–35. See also her subsequent

elaboration in *But She Said: Feminist Practices of Biblical Interpretation* (Boston: Beacon, 1992), 51–76.

64. For a fuller treatment, see Barbara Reid and Shelly Matthews, *Luke 10–24*, WCS 43B (Collegeville, MN: Liturgical Press, 2021), 353–61.

65. See, e.g., Bruce M. Metzger and Roland E. Murphy, eds., *The New Oxford Annotated Bible with the Apocryphal/Deuterocanonical Books* (New York: Oxford University Press, 1991), 98 NT.

66. See Bernadette Brooten, *Women Leaders in the Ancient Synagogue: Inscriptional Evidence and Background Issues*, BJS 36 (Chico, CA.: Scholars Press, 1982), who analyzes nineteen inscriptions that date from the first century BCE to the sixth century CE coming from synagogues in Asia Minor, Crete, Italy, Greece, Thrace, Egypt, and Palestine.

67. For excellent resources that help Christians better understand Jesus within Judaism, see Amy-Jill Levine, *The Misunderstood Jew: The Church and the Scandal of the Jewish Jesus* (San Francisco: Harper One, 2006); and *The Jewish Annotated New Testament*, ed. Amy-Jill Levine and Marc Zvi Brettler, rev. ed. (Oxford: Oxford University Press, 2017).

68. See, e.g., Luke 2:20; 7:22; 8:15, 21; 11:28 and comments above on Hearing and Acting on the Word as a characteristic of discipleship.

69. For an analysis of the questions about the provenance of Romans 16, see Joseph A. Fitzmyer, *Romans: A New Translation with Introduction and Commentary*, AYB 33 (New York: Doubleday, 1993), 55–67. Some scholars believe that Romans 16 was a separate letter originally destined for Ephesus and later added to the letter to the Romans.

70. Annette Bourland Huizenga (*1–2 Timothy, Titus*, WCS 53 [Collegeville, MN: Liturgical Press, 2016], 35) prefers "server," or "assistant."

71. Beverly Roberts Gaventa, "Romans," in *Women's Bible Commentary*, 3rd ed., 555.

72. Acts 18:11 notes that Paul spent eighteen months in Corinth. Paul's own letters indicate that he made at least one more trip there. Cenchreae was one of the two ports for the city of Corinth. See further Sojung Yoon, "Phoebe, a Minister in the Early Christian Church," in *Distant Voices Drawing Near. Essays in Honor of Antoinette Clark Wire*, ed. Holly E. Hearon (Collegeville, MN: Liturgical Press, 2004), 19–31.

73. See 1 Tim 5:3–16 for qualifications desired for those who are officially recognized as ministering widows in the early church.

74. Schüssler Fiorenza, *In Memory of Her*, 165–66.

75. An alternate interpretation is that *diakonein trapezais* refers not to eucharistic table service or food distribution but to financial administration. The Greek word *trapeza*, "table," is used for the table on which money changers do their transactions. In modern-day Greece, *trapeza* is the word for "bank." In this case, the ministry at issue in Acts 6 was akin to that of Mary Magdalene, Joanna, Susanna, and the other women in Luke 8:3 (see above).

76. Stephen, the first Hellenist chosen, is said to be full of the Holy Spirit (6:5), and the apostles' gesture of laying hands on the chosen seven while praying (6:6) could imply invocation of the Spirit, but the Spirit is not invoked in the decision-making process.

77. As I noted in my essay "The Power of Widows and How to Suppress It," in *A Feminist Companion to the Acts of the Apostles*, FCNTECW 9, ed. Amy-Jill Levine with Marianne Blickenstaff (London: T & T Clark, 2004), 85 n. 52, F. Scott Spencer ("Neglected Widows in Acts 6.1–7," *CBQ* 56 [1994]: 715–33), "argues that the twelve are ambivalent figures in the Lucan narrative, and their appraisal of the widows'

situation in Acts 6.1–7 shows the twelve not to be an entirely reliable voice. Their approach to needy widows is partly in line with the way that Jesus approaches widows with prayer and compassionate service, but it is also partly affiliated with the scribes, who deceitfully mix the practice of prayer with the neglect of widows. He sees a proclivity on the part of the twelve to promote the ministry of teaching and preaching at the expense of the service of food at table, in contrast to Jesus' pattern of blending the two vocations (Lk. 9.1–6, 10–17; 12.37–42; 17.7–10; 22.14–27). He sees a certain conversion on the part of Peter in the episode with Tabitha, where he combines prayer and service in an exemplary support system for needy widows. While I do not agree with Spencer that all Luke's widows were needy, I think he has important insights into the passage."

78. Huizenga, *1–2 Timothy, Titus*, 37.

79. These include Origen (early third century CE), John Chrysostom (late fourth century CE), Theodoret of Mopsuestia (late fourth century CE), Theodoret of Cyrrhus (early fifth century CE), and Pelagius (early fifth century CE). For more details, see Kevin Madigan and Carolyn Osiek, eds., *Ordained Women in the Early Church: A Documentary History* (Baltimore: Johns Hopkins University Press, 2005).

80. For more details, see Jennifer H. Stiefel, "Women Deacons in 1 Timothy: A Linguistic and Literary Look at 'Women Likewise…' (1 Tim 3:11)," in *Women Deacons? Essays with Answers*, ed. Phyllis Zagano (Collegeville, MN: Liturgical Press, 2016), 13–29.

81. Steifel, "Women Deacons," 28.

82. Steifel, "Women Deacons," 29.

83. See further Carolyn Osiek, "Women in House Churches," in *Common Life in the Early Church: Essays Honoring Graydon*

*F. Snyder*, ed. Julian V. Hills et al. (Harrisburg, PA: Trinity Press International, 1998), 300–315.

84. Margaret Dunlop Gibson, trans. and ed., *Didascalia (Teaching) of the Apostles in Syriac: Edited from a Mesopotamian Manuscript, with Various Readings and Collations of Other Mss* (London: C. J. Clay and Sons, 1903), as quoted by Huizenga, *1–2 Timothy, Titus*, 38.

85. For an excellent collection of essays that examine the biblical and historical evidence for women deacons from numerous perspectives with a view toward providing answers for the contemporary question concerning the ordination of women to the diaconate, see Phyllis Zagano, ed., *Women Deacons? Essays with Answers* (Collegeville, MN: Liturgical Press, 2016). See also the essays on "Women's Diaconate: Ecumenical Perspectives," in *Women in Church Ministries. Reform Movements in Ecumenism*, ed. Margit Eckholt, Dorothea Sattler, Ulrike Link-Wieczorek, and Andrea Strübind (Collegeville, MN: Liturgical Press, 2021), 77–127.

86. For detailed discussion on the historicity of the Twelve, see John P. Meier, *A Marginal Jew. Rethinking the Historical Jesus*, vol. 3: *Companions and Competitors*, ABRL (New York: Doubleday, 2001), 125–285.

87. Some mss. have seventy-two. Either way, it is symbolic of a full number. If seventy, both seven and ten are numbers signaling completeness (e.g., seven days of creation, Gen 1:1—2:3; ten commandments, Num 20:1–17) and multiplying seven by ten yields exponential fullness; if seventy-two, then it is seven times twelve, the full number of Israel's tribes.

88. The Greek word *andrōn* specifically refers to males, unlike *anthrōpōn*, which can be understood inclusive of males and females.

89. Rom 1:1; 11:13; 1 Cor 1:1; 9:1, 2; 15:9; 2 Cor 1:1; 12:12; Gal 1:1; Eph 1:1; Col 1:1; 1 Tim 1:1; 2:7; 2 Tim 1:1, 11; Tit 1:1.

90. See also Acts 14:4, 14.

91. Some scholars, such as Michael H. Burer and Daniel B. Wallace, "Was Junia Really an Apostle? A Re-examination of Rom 16.7," *NTS* 47 (2001): 76–91, interpret the phrase ***epistēmoi en tois apostolois*** to mean "well known to the apostles" rather than "prominent among the apostles." Linda L. Belleville, "'**Ιουνίαν…ἐπίσημοι ἐν τοῖς ἀποστόλοις**: A Re-examination of Romans 16.7 in Light of Primary Source Materials," *NTS* 51 (2005): 231–49, has shown that Hellenistic Greek literary works, papyri, inscriptions, and artifacts all show without exception that the phrase has the sense "notable among." This is also the meaning reflected in the interpretations of all patristic commentators.

92. Modern translations that opt for the feminine "Junia" include KJV, NAB, NRSV; choosing the masculine "Junias" are *La Biblia de las Américas*, NASB, NJB, and RSV. The RSV further interprets: "they are men of note among the apostles." The word *men* is not in the Greek text.

93. *In Epistolam ad Romanos*, Homilia 31, 2 (J. P. Migne, *Patrologiae cursus completus, series Graeca* [= PG] 60, 669–70).

94. For precise references, see Bernadette Brooten, "'Junia…Outstanding among the Apostles' (Romans 16:7)," in *Women Priests. A Catholic Commentary on the Vatican Declaration*, ed. Leonard Swidler and Arlene Swidler (New York: Paulist, 1977), 141–44.

95. See further Yii-Jan Lin, "Junia: An Apostle before Paul," *JBL* 139 (2020): 191–209; Jay Eldon Epp, *Junia: The First Woman Apostle* (Minneapolis: Fortress, 2005); Judette Gallares, "And She Will Speak: Junia, the Voice of a Silenced

Woman Apostle," in *Ecclesia of Women in Asia: Gathering the Voices of the Silenced*, ed. Evelyn Monteiro and Antoinette Gutzler, 89–107 (Delhi: ISPCK, 2005); Rena Pederson, *The Lost Apostle: Searching for the Truth about Junia* (San Francisco: Jossey-Bass, 2006).

96. Origen, *Comm. S. Jean* 4, 26–27. Another who calls her "apostle" is Theophylact of Bulgaria (ca. 1050–1108), archbishop of Ochrid and a biblical commentator. He also says she was "anointed with priesthood" (Joh. 4.28ff, MPG 123, 1241D).

97. In the Last Supper scene in John, those who are with Jesus are his "disciples," *mathētai*, a term used over seventy times in this Gospel for all those who are taught by and believe in Jesus. In contrast, Mark says it is the Twelve who are at table with Jesus (14:17); Matthew says the twelve disciples (26:20); in Luke, it is "the apostles" (22:14), whom Luke always identifies with the twelve (6:13; 9:1 with 9:10).

Although Matthew speaks of "twelve disciples" three times (10:1; 11:1; 28:16), presumably referring each time to the twelve men named at Matt 10:2, the twelve are not the only disciples Matthew has in view when he uses the term *mathētēs*, "disciple," which occurs seventy-three times. Joseph of Arimathea, e.g., is explicitly called a disciple at 27:57. Women, especially Mary Magdalene, Mary the mother of James and Joseph, and the mother of the sons of Zebedee, who witnessed Jesus's crucifixion, and who "had followed Jesus from Galilee and had provided for him" (28:55–56), are depicted as disciples, as we demonstrated above.

98. See Craig R. Koester, *Symbolism in the Fourth Gospel. Meaning, Mystery, Community*, 2nd ed. (Minneapolis: Fortress, 2003), 141–73.

99. Nicodemus will appear twice more (7:50; 19:39). In the scene at the burial, he demonstrates that he has indeed

come to full faith, as evident by the extravagant amount of spices he brings.

100. See, e.g., Rudolf Schnackenburg, *The Gospel According to St. John*, vol. 1: *Introduction and Commentary on Chapters 1–4* (New York: Crossroad, 1987), 432–33; Francis J. Moloney, *The Gospel of John*, SP 4 (Collegeville, MN: Liturgical Press, 1998), 127.

101. This is a favorite technique of the Fourth Evangelist. Another example is Mary Magdalene, who embodies the whole believing community as she goes alone to the tomb (20:1–2, 11–18). See further Raymond C. Collins, "Representative Figures of the Fourth Gospel," *DRev* 94 (1976): 118–32.

102. John Bligh, who proposed this interpretation decades ago ("Jesus in Samaria," *HeyJ* 3 [1962]: 336), notes, "There are in fact seven names, but as four of these occur in pairs, there are five idolatrous cults: Succothbenoth; Nergal; Ashima; Nibhaz and Tartak; Adrammelech and Anammelech. Josephus, wishing no doubt to simplify the narrative, says that five gods were imported" (*Ant.* IX, 288). While Bligh points the way, rightly, to a symbolic reading of the five husbands, he makes a curious interpretive move when he envisions the woman as speaking on a literal level about marriage and Jesus inviting her to a symbolic understanding. He thinks that when the woman replied *ouk echo andra*, "I have no man" (v. 17), "there was an element of deception in this, or at least of mental reservation. She had a man, though he was not her husband. Why then did she give this answer? She seems to desire to remain there alone with Christ…wanting, perhaps only half-consciously, marriage; he offers her instead the reality of which marriage is a figure." It is preferable to read the whole dialogue as taking place on a metaphorical, symbolic level, as does Sandra M. Schneiders, *Written That*

*You May Believe: Encountering Jesus in the Fourth Gospel*, rev. ed. (New York: Crossroad, 2003), 139.

Schneiders comments that the symbolic interpretation "has been regularly disputed by commentators who prefer the literal interpretation despite the context of the story and the high improbability that any Jew or Samaritan man would marry a woman who had been divorced several times" (139 n. 19).

103. Luise Schottroff, "The Samaritan Woman and the Notion of Sexuality in the Fourth Gospel," in "*What Is John?*," vol. 2: *Literary and Social Readings of the Fourth Gospel*, ed. Fernando F. Segovia, SymS 7 (Atlanta: Scholars Press, 1998), 157–81.

104. E.g., Moloney concludes, "Like Nicodemus she has arrived at a partial conditioned belief in Jesus" (*The Gospel of John*, 131). C. K. Barrett, *The Gospel According to St. John. An Introduction with Commentary and Notes on the Greek Text*, 2nd ed. (Philadelphia: Westminster, 1955), 228, sees the woman as "half convinced" when she goes into the city.

105. Mary Coloe, *God Dwells with Us: Temple Symbolism in the Fourth Gospel* (Collegeville, MN: Liturgical Press, 2001), 106.

106. John T. Squires, "An Informed Faith," https://johntsquires.com/2020/03/12/from-the-woman-at-the-well-to-a-byazantine-saint-john-4-st-photini-and-the-path-to-enlightenment/.

107. Kathleen Corley ("Slaves, Servants, and Prostitutes: Gender and Social Class in Mark," in *A Feminist Companion to Mark*, ed. Amy-Jill Levine with Marianne Blickenstaff, FCNTECW 2 (Sheffield: Sheffield Academic, 2001, 191–221) suggests that Mary the mother of James is Jesus's mother, recalling that in Mark 6:3, Jesus's brothers are said to be James and Joses and Judas and Simon (202). But earlier in

the Gospel (3:20–21, 31–35), Jesus's mother has opposed his ministry and seeks with other family members to "restrain" him, and then is rebuked by Jesus. In light of this, it seems unlikely that Mark intends us to understand the Mary in 15:40 as the mother of Jesus, since he does not tell of any change of heart on her part.

108. See the chart above, which shows the variation in each of the Gospels regarding the names of the women at the cross and tomb.

109. Most scholars consider 16:8 to be the original ending of the Gospel. The best Greek manuscripts, Sinaiticus and Vaticanus, end here. Two variants emerged in the second century, now dubbed "The Shorter Ending," which has no verse numbers, and "The Longer Ending" (16:9–20). In both, the style and vocabulary differ from that of Mark.

110. The verb *etheōroun*, "saw," is in the imperfect tense, emphasizing their continuing action as witnesses.

111. See Warren Carter, *Mark*, WCS 42 (Collegeville, MN: Liturgical Press, 2019), 446–53, for a summary of various interpretations offered by feminist scholars on 16:1–8.

112. See also the use of *proskynein*, "worship," or "do homage," in 2:8, where Herod says he wants to worship the newborn king, an action that the magi perform in 2:11; in 14:33, where Peter and the other disciples in the boat do worship Jesus after he walks on water; in 15:25 the Canaanite woman kneels before Jesus when she implores him to heal her daughter; in 28:17 the eleven disciples worship the risen Jesus on the mountain in Galilee to which he directed them.

113. Turid Karlsen Seim, *The Double Message: Patterns of Gender in Luke-Acts* (Nashville: Abingdon, 1994), 153, notes the following: expressions with *logos*: 8:15, 21; 10:39;11:28; *logoi*: 24:44; and *rhēmata*: 2:51; 24:8. See also Anne F. Elvey, *An Ecological Feminist Reading of the Gospel of*

*Luke: A Gestational Paradigm* (Lewiston, NY: Mellen, 2005), 137.

114. See also Exod 20:8; Num 15:39, 40; Deut 5:15; 15:15; 16:12; 24:18, 22, where remembering is accompanied by doing.

115. E.g., Gen 8:1; 9:15, 16; 19:29; 30:22; Exod 2:24; 6:5; Lev 26:42, 45; Num 10:9; 1 Sam 1:19.

116. It is found also at 1 Cor 11:24.

117. The above comments are excerpted and adapted from Barbara E. Reid, "The Gospel of Luke: Friend or Foe of Women Proclaimers of the Word?," *CBQ* 78 (2016): 19–22, a version of which also appears in Reid and Matthews, *Luke 1–9*, 633–36. As I noted in the latter (635 n. 28), "Another aspect of memory is explored by Carolyn Osiek ("The Women at the Tomb," 97–107). She examines the role and function of the women in the empty tomb stories using redaction criticism, social history, and social construction of meaning with regard to women's subcultures, burial customs, and public testimony. She shows that although the empty tomb story came to serve no kerygmatic purpose in the canonical tradition, the memory of the women's role was so persistent that it could not be removed. She concludes, 'Its very persistence must indicate that something actually happened that Sunday morning at the tomb'" (106). The opposite conclusion is reached by Kathleen E. Corley, *Maranatha: Women's Funerary Rituals and Christian Origins* (Minneapolis: Fortress, 2010), who argues that the empty tomb stories are late and fictional and that both the passion narratives and the resurrection traditions arose from women's storytelling in ritual laments."

118. As *lēros* is defined in BDAG, 594.

119. See Reid, *Choosing the Better Part?*, 202, 204. Mary Rose D'Angelo ("Women in Luke-Acts: A Redactional View," *JBL* 9, no. 3 [1992]: 441–61) demonstrated that in Luke no

woman speaks except to be corrected by Jesus (10:41–42; 11:27–28; 23:28) or to be disbelieved (24:11).

120. Seim, *Double Message*, 156.

121. While most commentators envision Cleopas's unnamed companion as a male, Sharon H. Ringe (*Luke*, Westminster Bible Companion [Louisville: Westminster John Knox, 1995], 286–87), sees them as a male-female missionary couple. For bibliography on the question, see J. Gillman, "The Emmaus Story in Luke-Acts Revisited," in *Resurrection in the New Testament: Festschrift J. Lambrecht*, ed. R. Bieringer, V. Kperski, and B. Lataire, BETL 165 (Leuven: Leuven University Press, 2002), 165–88. See also the icon by Sister Marie-Paul Farran, OSB: https://www.printeryhouse.org/ProdPage.asp?prod=M18.

122. See comments above, p. 113, n. 101, on Representative Characters in the Gospel of John. Note that Mary speaks in the first person plural, "we do not know where they have laid him" (20:2).

123. The Beloved Disciple, who also appears in the Last Supper scene as the one reclining at Jesus's breast (13:23–26), at the crucifixion (19:25–27), in the boat with the other disciples on the Sea of Tiberias (21:7), and in Jesus's dialogue with Peter in 21:20–23, is never named. This anonymity allows all disciples, female or male, to place themselves into the most intimate relationship with Jesus.

124. The following interpretation is based on Schneiders, *Written That You May Believe*, 202–23.

125. Not recognizing the risen Christ is a standard feature in resurrection appearance stories, as also with Cleopas and his companion in Luke 24:13–35.

126. There is an echo of John 10:3–5, where the Good Shepherd calls his sheep by name.

127. There are no punctuation marks in the Greek text. I concur with Sandra Schneiders (*Written That You May Believe*, 220), who reads 20:17 as a question, "Am I as yet (or still) not ascended?" The implied answer is "No, you are indeed ascended, that is, glorified." In the Fourth Gospel, there is no temporal sequence as in Luke, who has forty days of appearances between the resurrection and ascension, followed by ten more days between the ascension and Pentecost. In the Gospel of John, the passion, death, resurrection, ascension, glorification, and giving of the Spirit are all one moment, captured by the expression "the hour."

128. This is visibly demonstrated in the next scene. When the disciples are gathered in the evening of that first day behind locked doors, Jesus comes and stands in their midst (*eis to meson*, 20:19).

129. This annunciation becomes formulaic as the other disciples say to Thomas at 20:25, "We have seen the Lord."

130. For comments on how Luke attempts to suppress such traditions in order to advance his androcentric agenda, see Shelly Matthews, "Erasing Mary Magdalene: Traditions of Mary in the Fourth Gospel and Other Christian Literature of Which Luke Will Not Speak," in Reid and Matthews, *Luke 10–24*, 636–38.

131. See Karen L. King, "The Gospel of Mary Magdalene," in *Searching the Scriptures: A Feminist Commentary*, vol. 2, ed E. Schüssler Fiorenza (New York: Crossroad, 1994), 601–34.

132. Hippolytus of Rome, *Commentary on the Song of Songs* 25.6, 7. Many scholars think he is referring to Mary Magdalene, but it is also possible he was speaking of Mary and Martha of Bethany. See Mary Ann Beavis, "Reconsidering Mary of Bethany," *CBQ* 74 (2012): 281–97.

133. See further "Excavating Migdal/Reconstructing Mary," in Reid and Matthews, *Luke 1–9*, 255–57.

134. See Elizabeth Schrader and Joan E. Taylor, "The Meaning of 'Magdalene': A Review of Literary Evidence," *JBL* 140 (2021): 751–73.

135. See Jane Schaberg, "How Mary Magdalene Became a Whore," *BibRev* 8 (1992): 30–37, 51–52; Schaberg, *The Resurrection of Mary Magdalene: Legends, Apocrypha, and the Christian Testament* (New York: Continuum, 2004).

136. For the text of his homily, see Reid and Matthews, *Luke 1–9*, 257–58.

137. See Matthijs den Dulk, "I Permit No Woman to Teach Except for Thecla: The Curious Case of the Pastoral Epistles and the Acts of Paul Reconsidered," *NovT* 54 (2012): 176–203.

138. Sheila E. McGinn, "The Acts of Thecla," in *Searching the Scriptures*, vol. 2: *A Feminist Commentary*, ed. Elisabeth Schüssler Fiorenza with the assistance of Ann Brock and Shelly Matthews (New York: Crossroad, 1994), notes that "looking like a man may have provided an additional measure of safety in travel. Further, female dress styles are more constricting that men's—and often seem designed expressly for that purpose (e.g., the practice of foot binding and its modern equivalent—high heeled shoes). Dresses are impractical for travel, whether on foot or horseback, and long hair is difficult to maintain when one spends much time in the open air. Pragmatic issues such as these may have had at least as much to do with the decision to dress 'like a man' as did any putative desire to abandon one's female nature" (828 n. 94).

139. See Stephen J. Davis, *The Cult of St. Thecla: A Tradition of Women's Piety in Late Antiquity*, OECS (New York: Oxford University Press, 2001).

140. "Protomartyr and Equal of the Apostles Thekla," in Orthodox Church in America (September 24, 2020), https://www.oca.org/saints/lives/2020/09/24/102715-protomartyr-and-equal-of-the-apostles-thekla.

141. For further exploration of Thecla and her significance, see Sheila E. McGinn's forthcoming monograph *Exploring the Acts of Thecla* in the Rhetoric of Religious Antiquity series from SBL Press. See also Susan E. Hylen, *A Modest Apostle: Thecla and the History of Women in the Early Church* (New York: Oxford University Press, 2015).

142. "Saint Nino (Nina), Equal of the Apostles, Enlightener of Georgia," in Orthodox Church in America (January 14, 2019), https://www.oca.org/index.php/saints/lives/2017/01/14/100191-saint-nino-nina-equal-of-the-apostles-enlightener-of-georgia.

## III

1. Osiek and MacDonald, *A Woman's Place*, 163.

2. Acts 9:36–43 leaves many questions unanswered. It is not clear whether Tabitha/Dorcas was herself a widow, what was her precise relationship to the widows mourning her death, and whether the clothing they made was given out as part of Tabitha's charitable works (Acts 9:36), or whether this work was her means of support. See further Amy-Jill Levine, "Tabitha/Dorcas: Spinning Off Cultural Criticism," in *Delightful Acts: New Essays on Canonical and Non-canonical Acts*, ed. Harold W. Attridge, Dennis R. MacDonald, Clare K. Rothschild, WUNT 391 (Tübingen: Mohr Siebeck, 2017), 41–65.

3. Several manuscripts do not have the phrase "into her home" (as reflected in the NAB translation). To end v. 38 with "welcomed him" is abrupt and incomplete. It is most

likely that the clause "into her home" originally concluded the verse. There is no apparent motive for deleting "into her home" except to downplay Martha's role as host of a house church. See further Bruce M. Metzger, *A Textual Commentary on the Greek New Testament: A Companion Volume to the United Bible Societies' Greek New Testament (Third Edition)* (London: United Bible Societies, 1971), 153. See also Kathleen Corley, *Private Women, Public Meals: Social Conflict in the Synoptic Tradition* (Peabody, MA: Hendrickson, 1993), 134–35.

4. See comments above, p. 119, n. 123, on the anonymity and function of the Beloved Disciple.

5. This section is adapted from Reid and Matthews, *Luke 10–24*, 421–34.

6. Jesus was not unique in criticizing socially discriminatory dining practices. See Martial, *Epigrams* 1.20; 3.60; Juvenal, *Satires* 5; Pliny, *Letters* 2.6.

7. Louise A. Gosbell, *"The Poor, the Crippled, the Blind, and the Lame": Physical and Sensory Disability in the Gospels of the New Testament*, WUNT 469 (Tübingen: Mohr Siebeck, 2018), 185.

8. Dennis E. Smith, "Table Fellowship as a Literary Motif in the Gospel of Luke," *JBL* 106 (1987): 613–38, here 617; see photos and reconstructions in Smith, *From Symposium to Eucharist: The Banquet in the Early Christian World* (Minneapolis: Fortress, 2003), 15–17.

9. Elisabeth Schüssler Fiorenza, "'Waiting at Table': A Critical Feminist Theological Reflection on Diakonia," *Concilium 198. Diakonia: Church for the Others*, ed. N. Breinacher and N. Mette (Edinburgh: T & T Clark, 1988), 84–94.

10. See Luke 5:27–39; 7:36–50; 9:10–17; 10:38–42; 11:37–54; 14:1–24; 19:1–10; 22:14–38; 24:13–35 and 24:36–43. Many of these are unique to Luke.

11. On meals in Luke as philosophical banquets, see Smith, *From Symposium to Eucharist*, 253–72.

12. Luke 5:29–32; 7:36–50; 11:37–54; 14:1–24; 22:14–38. On women and meals in the Gospel of Luke, see Corley, *Private Women, Public Meals*, 108–46.

13. For references and more detail, see Corley, *Private Women, Public Meals*, 53–66.

14. *Therapeutae* means "attendants," those who attend the gods or God (Joan E. Taylor, *Jewish Women Philosophers of First-Century Alexandria: Philo's "Therapeutae" Reconsidered* [Oxford: Oxford University Press, 2003], 343).

15. Philo, *Vit. Cont.* 83, describes how men and women join in singing after the meal, leaving their separate places where they have reclined for the meal and forming two choirs for the singing. Taylor, *Jewish Women Philosophers*, 287.

16. Osiek and MacDonald, *A Woman's Place*, 161.

17. Corley, *Private Women, Public Meals*, 144–46. See also Osiek and MacDonald, *A Woman's Place*, 161–62, on resistance to women teachers.

## IV

1. Letty M. Russell, *Church in the Round: Feminist Interpretation of the Church* (Louisville, KY: Westminster/John Knox Press, 1993).

2. See Cardinal Joseph W. Tobin, "The Long Game," *Commonweal* (June 2021): 24–27.

3. See Barbara E. Reid. "Synodal and Collegial Thinking and Acting in the New Testament," *Concilium* 2 (2021): 59–67.

4. See, e.g., Margaret J. Wheatley, *Leadership and the New Science: Discovering Order in a Chaotic World*, 3rd ed. (San Francisco: Berrett-Koehler, 2006).

5. See, e.g., Peter Block, *Community: The Structure of Belonging* (San Francisco: Berrett-Koehler, 2008); Ronald Heifetz, Alexander Grashow, Marty Linsky, *The Practice of Adaptive Leadership: Tools and Tactics for Changing Your Organization and the World* (Cambridge: Cambridge Leadership Associates, 2009).

6. Donna Markham, *Spiritlinking Leadership: Working through Resistance to Organizational Change* (Mahwah, NJ: Paulist, 1999).

## V

1. As a headline in Global Sisters Report of the *National Catholic Reporter* declared, January 7, 2016, https://www.globalsistersreport.org/news/trends/sr-madeleva-wolff-forever-changed-face-catholic-theology-36166.